A BODLEY HEAD ARCHAEOLOGY

Introducing Archaeology

MAGNUS MAGNUSSON

Drawings by
MARTIN SIMMONS

THE BODLEY HEAD · London Sydney Toronto

UNIFORM WITH THIS BOOK

RONALD HARKER *Digging Up the Bible Lands*
T. G. H. JAMES *The Archaeology of Ancient Egypt*
REYNOLD HIGGINS *Minoan Crete*
MAGNUS MAGNUSSON *Viking Expansion Westwards*
JOHN HAY *Ancient China*

IN PREPARATION

BARRY CUNLIFFE *Rome and the Barbarians*
DAVID BROWN *The Archaeology of Anglo-Saxon England*
PETER HARBISON *The Archaeology of Ireland*
ANNA RITCHIE *The Archaeology of Early Scotland*
KENNETH HUDSON *World Industrial Archaeology*

FRONTISPIECE
Layard sketching in the ruins of
Nineveh during the excavation
of the mound of Kuyunjik.
A drawing by S. C. Malan, 1852.

© Magnus Magnusson, 1972
Drawings © The Bodley Head Ltd 1972
ISBN 0 370 01568 1
Printed and bound in Great Britain for
The Bodley Head Ltd
9 Bow Street, London WC2E 7AL
by Tindal Press Ltd, Chelmsford
Set in Monophoto Ehrhardt by
BAS Printers Limited, Wallop, Hampshire
First published 1972
Reprinted 1974

CONTENTS

ACKNOWLEDGMENTS

Thanks are due to the following for permission to reproduce black and white photographs:
The Mansell Collection, Frontispiece, pages 34, 37; Universitetets Oldsaksamling, Oslo, page 9; the Trustees of the British Museum, pages, 16, 41, 43, 45, 65, 66, 83; Peter Clayton, pages 18, 20, 21, 24, 29, 31, 55, 58, 63, 98; Aerofilms Ltd., page 23; the Peabody Museum, Cambridge, Massachusetts, page 50; Department of Egyptology, University College London, page 61; Dr. G. H. S. Bushnell, page 69; the Griffith Institute, Ashmolean Museum, Oxford, pages 73, 75, 76; the Society for Cultural Relations with the USSR, page 78; Miss B. Wagstaff, page 82; Josephine Powell, page 87; Eric de Maré, page 91; Robert Stenuit, page 94; UNESCO, London, pages 99, 100; Edwin C. Rockwell, Jr. for a photograph taken in the Ancient Bristlecone Pine Forest in the Inyo National Forest, California, page 105; the Trustees of the British Museum (Natural History), page 112; the Smithsonian Institution, Washington, D.C., page 116; the Metropolitan Museum of Art, New York, page 119; the Vindolanda Trust, page 122.

Thanks are due to the following for coloured photographs:
Universitetets Oldsaksamling, Oslo, facing page 32; Peter Clayton, jacket photograph, and facing pages 33, 48 (bottom), 81; Dr. G. H. S. Bushnell, facing page 49; the Earl of Elgin, facing page 48 (top); the Trustees of the British Museum, facing pages 80, 96 (top); Roskilde Museum, Denmark, facing page 96 (bottom); the Camelot Research Committee, facing page 97 (top); UNESCO, Paris, facing page 97 (bottom).

The drawing on page 15 is based on material in possession of the British Museum; the plan on page 38 is based on that on page 8 of the British Museum's handbook, *Assyrian Palace Reliefs;* the drawing on page 40 is based on a diagram on page 20 in the British Museum's handbook, *An Historical Guide to the Sculptures of the Parthenon.*

1

What is archaeology?

I call it my talisman, my lucky token, and it always sits on the desk in front of me. It is my most treasured possession; and yet it is worth nothing at all—just an ordinary stone, about the size and shape of a pear. It was given to me some fifteen years ago by a parish priest on the Hebridean island of South Uist when I was a young reporter on a newspaper; and although I cannot now remember what the story I was covering was about, I have never forgotten the gift of the stone.

It had been found, so I was told, during the excavation of an archaeological site on South Uist near a tiny crofting village called Kilpheder, which stands on a long stretch of low-lying fertile grassland called *machair* in Gaelic—a carpet of rich, springy turf on top of sand-dunes. It was a very old site, and had been buried under the sand for many centuries. It turned out to be an ancient homestead of the type known as a 'wheel-house' because its design was just like that of a wheel: a round house with room-partitions like the spokes of a wheel radiating from a central hub. These houses were occupied by a people called the Picts about 1500 years ago—the Picts had been living in Scotland for many centuries before the 'Scots' as we know them today arrived and took over the country.

The stone I was given was found on the floor of one of the chambers of the wheel-house at Kilpheder. Both ends of the stone, the blunt end and the sharper end, showed signs of having been chipped; and on the surface of the stone were some irregular dark patches, like grease-marks. When I hold the stone in my hand, these grease-marks fit exactly the flesh-pads of my palm and fingers, because these dark marks, I was assured, had been made by sweat; they were the grimy sweat-marks of people who had used the stone as a primitive hammer all those long centuries ago.

To hold this stone in my own hand gave me then, and gives me still, a shiver of excitement. It works as a kind of time-machine that transports me suddenly and vividly into the intimate physical presence of the Pictish families who lived and died in that huddled, sunken house. These were not the wild and painted savages the Roman historians portrayed so patronisingly when the legions invaded Scotland; these were ordinary peaceful farmers who grazed their livestock on the *machair*, grew corn which they ground into flour for bread, caught fish—and used handy stones from the seashore as improvised hammers.

Because this pear-shaped stone with its lingering sweat-marks brings these long-dead people to life in a way that no history textbook could do, it symbolises for me all the fascination of archaeology. Fundamentally, archaeology is simply a way of getting closer to the people of the past, our ancestors. It can be defined as the systematic study and interpretation of antiquities as a means of reconstructing the story of man from material remains. It involves anything and everything left over from the past, all the tangible, visible things that man has left behind him—the things he made with his hands (*artifacts*, or artificial products), the houses he lived in, the graves he buried his dead in, the books he wrote and the tablets he inscribed, the temples he worshipped in. The actual objects the archaeologist studies and 'reads' include everything from imposing monuments like an Egyptian pyramid to the meanest mud hut, from the most brilliant treasures to the most insignificant piece of discarded garbage, from the most solid remains like Stonehenge to the merest shadows in the soil.

And this 'past' includes every period of time from the earliest beginnings of man half a million years ago right down to the twentieth century, for today's present is tomorrow's yesterday; and already there is a widespread and growing interest in 'industrial archaeology', which seeks to study, record, and if possible preserve the physical remains of the great technological and economic revolution in industry that really ushered in the modern era for western Europe. So archaeology is as much concerned with an early beam-engine as with a Viking ship-burial; and through the development of new science-based techniques, it is as much concerned with carbon atoms and ancient pollen-seeds as with the spectacular ruins

The Oseberg Ship
during excavation,
September, 1904. The
steering paddle is in
position at the stern,
nearest the camera.

of classical antiquity. The range of archaeology seems inexhaustible, and everything is grist to the archaeologist's mill, whether it is above the ground or under the ground or even under the sea.

Archaeology is a branch of history, in the sense in which history means a study of the past. But archaeologists use the word *history* in a special sense as well, meaning an account of the past based on written records. The period before written records began is called *prehistory;* and *protohistory* is the term used to cover the period between *prehistory* and *history*, when occasional written records might be available but before fully written history began. Archaeology clearly has a part to play in all these periods. In *prehistory* it is the major source of our knowledge, building up a picture of a society or a culture, from the surviving material evidence. In *protohistory* it is still a major source of information, to supplement what meagre

9

and oblique written records there might be. In *history* proper, archaeology provides a valuable complement to the written records, helping to give the people of the past a physical and social context.

Let us look at one example, from the protohistory of Scandinavia, of the way in which archaeology and written records can combine to create a more rounded and imaginative picture of the past than either can do separately.

In 1904, a Viking ship was excavated from a burial mound at Oseberg, in the south of Norway. It was a beautiful ninth-century boat, lavishly decorated with woodcarvings; not a pirate longship like the Gokstad ship that had been excavated nearby some twenty years earlier, but an elegant State barge. It had a large burial chamber amidships, which had been broken into and practically stripped by grave-robbers not many years after the funeral. The chamber had had two occupants, whose skeletons were found despoiled nearby. One skeleton was that of a woman of about fifty, whose hands and arms had been mutilated, doubtless in order to wrench off her rings and golden bracelets; the other was of a woman of about thirty, presumably a slave. In the ship were found the remains of all the appropriate furniture and equipment for a royal progress to the next world: a four-wheeled cart, four sledges, two beds with bedding, tapestries, looms, buckets, casks, chests, kitchen utensils, cauldrons, cooking-pots, and a complete skeleton of an ox, riding harness and sundry personal possessions. But nothing was left of any precious stones or metals.

Most of the objects had been shattered by the stones that had been thrown into the ship to anchor it in its mound, and required the most careful reconstruction to restore them. But the ship itself had been wonderfully preserved for more than a thousand years in a mound of blue clay covered with peaty soil, and is now on display in the Viking Ship Museum in Oslo.

But although the ship and its contents were marvellous examples of Viking art, they were essentially museum pieces, dead objects that archaeology had brilliantly recovered from the ground. For the ship to come alive again, it needed the presence of identifiable people from the pages of history. It had obviously been the burial mound of a Norse queen—but who was the rich and powerful queen whose body had been so unceremoniously abused after her funeral? The neighbouring Gokstad ship, too, had been used for a noble funeral, and that too had been plundered. Inside the burial chamber there was a skeleton of a fifty-year-old man well over six feet tall who had suffered so severely from gout in the left leg that he must have been half-paralysed. Who was he?

It was the Icelandic Sagas that supplied the possible answers; in particular, the great 'History of the Kings of Norway' known as *Heimskringla* (Orb of the World), written by the thirteenth-century Icelandic historian Snorri Sturluson. In it he describes the proto-history of Norway, that misty period in the ninth century between legend and history proper. And one of the memorable characters he describes is the redoubtable Queen 'Asa.

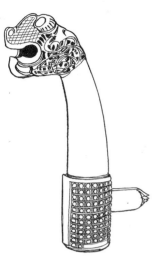

Animal head post from the Oseberg Ship

She was the daughter of the king of Agdir, and as a young and beautiful princess she caught the fancy of the elderly king of neighbouring Vestfold—Gudröd the Hunting King. When 'Asa refused his offer of marriage he made a raid on Agdir, killed her father and brother, and carried her off by force. Soon they had a son called Halfdan—Halfdan the Black; but this by no means reconciled Asa to her fate. Her opportunity for revenge came a year after Halfdan's birth. King Gudröd was exceptionally drunk one evening, and 'Asa got her personal servant to murder him as he staggered off his ship. Next morning, having acknowledged the killing, she sailed back to Agdir with her baby son. There she brought him up to take over his grandfather's kingdom of Agdir; and meanwhile, the kingdom of Vestfold was inherited by Gudröd's twenty-year-old son by a previous marriage, Olaf.

All this happened around 840 AD. Eighteen years later, Halfdan the Black took over the throne of Agdir, and came to an amicable arrangement with his half-brother Olaf whereby they divided between them the kingdom of Vestfold. Olaf would be about forty years old by then; the date, around 860 AD. Some time later, says Snorri Sturluson in *Heimskringla*, Olaf fell ill. He was staying near Gokstad when he developed such severe gout that he died, and was buried in the district of Geirstadir (Gjekstad), which includes Gokstad. There can be little doubt that the gouty skeleton in the Gokstad ship is that of Olaf.

And the Oseberg ship? After Olaf's death Halfdan the Black took over the whole of Vestfold; he spent the next twenty years in constant warfare, carving out a more sizeable kingdom in Norway which he handed over in turn to his son, the man who was to become the first king to unite the whole of Norway under one crown late in the ninth century—King Harald Fine-Hair. So Queen 'Asa was, in effect, the grandmother of modern Norway. It is not known exactly when she died; but the Oseberg ship was buried around 870 AD, like the Gokstad ship, when 'Asa would have been about fifty years old, and we know of no other royal lady of similar stature in Norway at this time. Besides, the name Oseberg seems too like "'Asa's berg' to be a coincidence.

However compelling and attractive the evidence, nevertheless the association of the ships with 'Asa and Olaf must remain a conjecture, an act of judgement, a hypothesis based on informed opinion. And this is the nature of all archaeology. This is what helps make archaeology so endlessly interesting. There are no absolutes. There is always a chance that a theory, no matter how carefully argued or long accepted, will be utterly destroyed by one chance new discovery. Archaeology involves a constantly fluid and flexible interpretation of available evidence; it is a book that is never closed. It takes immense skill and knowledge to be a good archaeologist, both during the excavation of a site and in the interpretation of the evidence to form a coherent picture; and archaeologists constantly have to discipline themselves against the excitement of discovery; they have to school themselves to be cautious and very precise in their deductions. There is an old adage about interpreting material remains unearthed during excavation: one stone is a stone, two stones are to be respected, three stones are a feature—but four stones are a wall!

Kitchen utensils from the Oseberg Ship

This half-serious slogan illustrates the kind of approach the professional archaeologist has to adopt. Like a good detective, he must not miss anything, however insignificant or unimportant it might seem at the time, and he must be prepared to be endlessly patient. He has to be armed, nowadays, with a formidable battery of skills; he needs to have a working knowledge of many other allied subjects, he needs to be able to use the latest scientific aids intelligently, he needs an encyclopaedic knowledge of his chosen field to make the inspired connections and associations that often lead to illumination and discovery.

It is, essentially, a professional activity. But that does not mean that amateurs have no part to play in it. They can take part in excavations as volunteer diggers under expert supervision and get to know a great deal about how to interpret evidence. Capable enthusiasts are always welcome at excavations if they are prepared to work hard and seriously, and there are countless societies throughout the country where the novice, whether young or old, can learn enough to make himself useful.

But quite apart from being useful to archaeology, the amateur can find archaeology useful to himself. It has, as I have tried to suggest, a profound fascination for people—and this is because it is ultimately about people. One of the most distinguished of British archaeologists, Sir Mortimer Wheeler, put it like this:

> 'The archaeological excavator is not digging up *things*, he is digging up *people;* however much he may analyse and tabulate and dessicate his discoveries in the laboratory, the ultimate appeal across the ages, whether the time-interval be 500 or 500,000 years, is from mind to intelligent mind, from man to sentient man . . . . Too often we dig up mere things, unrepentantly forgetful that our proper aim is to dig up people.' (*Archaeology from the Earth*)

Geoffrey Bibby, who has been looking for traces of the Biblical legend of the Garden of Eden on the little island of Bahrein in the Arabian Gulf, put it slightly differently:

> 'Every archaeologist knows in his heart why he digs. He digs, in pity and humility, that the dead may live again, that what is past may not be forever lost, that something may be salvaged from the wreck of ages.' (*The Testimony of the Spade*)

Through archaeology we relive the great and small dramas of the past, the fate of civilisations and the individuals who belonged to them and created them. We learn about them not only through the remains of great monuments like the Parthenon in Athens, but also through the incidental, accidental bric-à-brac of life and death—a child's toy, a broken comb, a layer of ash, a mislaid spindle-whorl, a necklace in a grave, or a sweat-marked pear-shaped stone. All these bring us into personal contact with people who had the same hopes and fears and ambitions as ourselves, people we can recognise as ourselves.

'What's past is prologue,' wrote Shakespeare in *The Tempest*. We look to the past because it contains the seeds of the future, as well as providing us with our identity as human beings. But considering how long is the span of time covered by archaeology, it is astonishing to realise that all the knowledge about the past that archaeology has already given us, all the knowledge of great civilisations that had vanished apparently without trace, has been achieved in a very short space of time. Archaeology, which we now take so much for granted, is really a very young subject.

2

The Early History of Archaeology

THE FIRST 'ARCHAEOLOGISTS'

In his great palace at Nineveh, King Ashurbanipal of Assyria (668–627 BC), grandson of the terrible Sennacherib who fell upon Jerusalem 'like a wolf on the fold', built up a library of over 20,000 'books' in the form of clay tablets. He sent his scribes to every corner of the Assyrian empire to copy and translate any old writings they came across, and he commissioned the production of grammars and dictionaries. Yet it is only just over a century ago, in 1854, that this magnificent library was discovered in the ruins of Nineveh; and another twenty years passed before it was realised that one of the 'books', the so-called Epic of Gilgamesh, contained an ancient version of a Great Flood story that bore striking resemblances to the story of Noah in the Old Testament book of *Genesis*. The discovery of the library and the gradual decipherment of its contents led archaeologists to the discovery of the completely lost Sumerian civilisation of Mesopotamia; so we owe a great debt of gratitude to King Ashurbanipal for being the earliest 'conservationist' we know of!

The first 'archaeologist' known to history was also a king: King Nabonidus, the father of Belshazzar, who ruled the Babylonian empire from 555–538 BC. He had a strange hobby for a warrior king; he liked excavating ruined temples from earlier times, and collecting old inscriptions. One of the ruins he excavated—and restored—was the ziggurat, or tower, of the ancient Mesopotamian city of Ur of the Chaldees, known to us from the Bible as the birthplace of Abraham. When the site of Ur was first excavated in the 1850's, some boxes were found amongst the foundations of the ziggurat, and inside these boxes were inscribed cylinders which announced that King

Sir Leonard Woolley's
reconstruction of the
ziggurat at Ur, as it
would have been after
restoration by King
Nabonidus in about
530 BC

Nabonidus of Babylon had made exploratory excavations in the ruins of the ziggurat and studied the records left by the original builders: 'The ziggurat is very old. I restored this ziggurat to its former state with mortar and baked bricks.' And as a mark of respect to his predecessor, he had the name of the original builder carved on a tablet and given a place of honour in the restored building: Ur-Nammu. Nabonidus, in fact, was doing precisely what many modern archaeologists do today—trying to restore a ruined building to a greater or lesser extent to allow posterity to see what it had once been like. King Nabonidus was a 'preservationist'.

Similarly, his daughter, the Princess En-nigaldi-Nannar, pursued another important branch of archaeology. Like all Babylonian princesses she was a temple priestess, but she seems to have inherited her father's antiquarian interests. When Sir Leonard Woolley excavated the site of Ur of the Chaldees in the 1920s, he found a little annexe to the temple, and in this annexe Princess En-nigaldi-Nannar had kept a collection of antiquities from the southern states of Mesopotamia. She had gone to the trouble of copying out an older inscription on a clay cylinder—'the oldest museum label known', as Sir Leonard called it, which makes the Princess the earliest museum-keeper we know of.

But to call this kind of activity 'archaeology' would be a misnomer. It was the ancient Greeks who invented the word *archaeology*,

15

meaning simply 'the discussion of antiquities'. In English the word now has the more specialised meaning of 'the scientific study of the material remains and monuments of the past'. The ancient Greeks certainly had a concept of the history of civilisation, and the poet Hesiod wrote in *Works and Days* of five successive Ages of the world, each one worse than the last; but this is myth rather than history, echoing the Biblical concept of a fall from grace. The Greeks did not pursue archaeology in the modern sense; their writers and historians were often widely travelled men, like Herodotus in the fifth century BC, careful observers who have left us fascinating accounts of how their less civilised neighbours lived; but no attempt seems to have been made to build a systematic picture of the past.

A clay cylinder that belonged to Princess En-nigaldi-Nannar, found in a temple at Ur. Inscribed on it is a copy from a much earlier inscription, also found at Ur. Called by Sir Leonard Woolley 'the oldest museum label'.

In fact, archaeology in the modern sense of the term only began to develop seriously during the eighteenth century, and there were many factors that contributed to it and helped to shape its beginnings. The Renaissance of the fifteenth century had stimulated curiosity in the rediscovered writings and monuments of classical antiquity, and it became fashionable to collect ancient works of art; many of these early collections eventually formed the basis of the great museums of Europe—the Louvre in Paris, for instance, was created after the French Revolution out of the forfeited royal collections of the Bourbon dynasty. The taste for collecting created a market that encouraged the deliberate exploration of ancient sites in search of valuable artifacts. And as the Muslim grip on the Bible lands slackened, more and more scholars travelled to the Near East in search of Biblical antiquities.

THE ENGLISH ANTIQUARIANS

Meanwhile, in England local antiquaries began to take an interest in the prehistory of Britain itself, the dark centuries before the arrival of the Romans of which nothing was known except the accounts of the Roman historians and the vast surviving monuments like Stonehenge in Wiltshire. The first general guide to the antiquities of Britain, under the nationalistic title of *Britannia*, was published by William Camden as early as 1586; Camden (1551–1623), who was headmaster of Westminster School, had travelled extensively throughout England, and *Britannia* contains a mass of antiquarian and topographical material and illustrations of ancient monuments. He was a pioneer of what he called 'back looking curiousity', and his studies reflected and pleased the intellectual atmosphere of sixteenth-century England—self-confidently patriotic and looking to a nationalistic identity in terms of the priestly caste of Druids described by the Roman chroniclers as having fiercely resisted the invaders.

John Aubrey of Wiltshire (1626–97) was another English antiquarian to be fired with the idea of England's barbarian but noble past. It was he who first noticed the 56 mysterious Aubrey Holes that surround Stonehenge. He declared firmly that Stonehenge was pre-Roman; in his eyes, the Ancient Britons 'were two or three degrees I suppose less savage than the Americans'.

William Stukeley (1687–1765) lived at a time when antiquarian societies were being founded all over England, and he lent all his considerable authority to the romantic view of the Druids as the builders of Stonehenge. Modern scholarship shows him to have been wrong, but the careful drawings and descriptions he made of these prehistoric monuments are of exceptional value today, for he was an accurate observer and has left us a clear record of what Stonehenge and Avebury, for instance, looked like in the eighteenth century. They were remarkable men, these busy and dedicated pioneers; more often than not wrong, frequently amusingly wrong, but they

The title page of
William Camden's
Britannia, 1607
edition.

were at least the forerunners of the habit of precise observation and recording that modern archaeology demands, and with their scholarly enthusiasm they were laying the foundations for more scientific studies. Above all, they had a lofty serenity which reads well even to this day. William Camden, for instance: 'In the study of Antiquity (which is always accompanied with dignity and hathe a certaine resemblance with eternity) there is a sweet food of the mind well befitting such as are of honest and noble disposition.' Or John Aubrey, despite the fact that a contemporary called him 'magotie-headed': 'These Remaines are *tamquam Tabulata Naufragy* (like fragments of a shipwreck) that after the Revolution of so many Yeares and Governments have escaped the Teeth of Time and (which is more dangerous) the Hands of mistaken Zeale. So that the retrieving of these Things from Oblivion in some sort resembles the Art of the Conjuror, who makes those walke and appeare that have layen in their graves many hundreds of yeares; and to represent to the eye, the places, Customs and Fashions that were of old Times.'

Drawing from Camden's *Britannia*, 1607, of a cross said to have been found in King Arthur's grave

The eighteenth century saw the start of the retrieving of these 'Things from Oblivion' on a large scale. In 1776 the Duke of Northumberland attempted an excavation of Silbury Hill in Wiltshire, the largest man-made prehistoric mound in Europe—it stands 130 feet high and covers just over 5 acres at the base. John Aubrey had described it and sketched it; so had William Stukeley, and both had recorded local traditions that it was the burial mound of a King Zel and contained a lifesize statue of the king on horseback in solid gold. So the Duke of Northumberland imported some tin-miners from Cornwall, who dug a vertical shaft eight feet square from the flat top of the mound right down to the original ground surface 130 feet below. But he was no more successful at finding a rich burial at the heart of the mound than the highly sophisticated excavation by tunnelling that was carried out in 1968–9!

EARLY EXCAVATIONS

The first excavations were unashamedly treasure-hunts. Early in the eighteenth century, shafts were sunk through the compacted volcanic ash from Mount Vesuvius that had engulfed the Roman city of Herculaneum in 79 AD—the same eruption that had also destroyed Pompeii. The workmen had instructions to smash through anything that stood in the way of their search for classical statuary; and for seven years they plundered this fine site relentlessly. But a few decades later, Charles of Bourbon, King of the Two Sicilies, had the shafts reopened under the supervision of a trained scholar who translated the inscriptions he found and attempted a systematic study. The search for Pompeii followed the same pattern: ruthless destruction by a hired gang of convicts in the heedless pursuit of treasure in 1748 was succeeded by a properly supervised exploration run by the great German-born art historian, Johann Winckelmann (1717–68), who published the first comprehensive historical account of classical art.

A British druid. An illustration from William Stukeley's *Stonehenge: a Temple Restored to the British Druids*, 1740.

Winckelmann is one of a number of antiquarians who have been given the honorary title of 'the father of archaeology'. But Sir Mortimer Wheeler has made the happy suggestion that the first scientific archaeological excavator of modern times was no less a person than Thomas Jefferson, the third President of the United States of America and co-author of the Declaration of Independence.

In 1784, Jefferson excavated an Indian mound in Virginia because he had a particular interest in ethnology and wanted to put to the test various theories and traditions about this particular site. His report on that excavation was a model of objective observation and sober deduction. He noted that it was a community grave, and that the bones had been deposited in four strata, or layers, separated by earth and stones; these layers seemed unconnected with each other, and he deduced they had been buried at different times. He noted that some of the dead had been children, because of the presence of the rib of an infant and part of the jaw of a child that had not yet cut its teeth. He noted that some of the stones had been brought from some distance away. He noted that none of the bones had been obviously mutilated by weapons, and he concluded that the mound was not, as had been previously supposed, a war cemetery to house the bodies of warriors killed in some battle.

Part of the great stone circle of Avebury from William Stukeley's *Abury: a Temple of the British Druids*, 1743.

A peice of the great circle or Allien at the South Entrance into the temple at Abury Aug 1724.

Jefferson, the inspired amateur, was years ahead of his time. A hundred years later, most archaeologists were still not applying the principles of excavation and deduction that he had used quite instinctively. It was to take a long time for archaeology to cease to be a matter of treasure-hunting rather than a search for objective truth about the past.

THE FIRST TIME-SCALE

But in Scandinavia a more scholarly approach was beginning to develop by the early decades of the nineteenth century, when attempts were made to place discovered objects and monuments in a meaningful time-scale—to work out what came first, and when. From these studies emerged the first clear classification of man's antiquity, the cornerstone of our reading of prehistory—a broad sequence based on three major technological Ages of Man: the Stone Age, the Bronze Age, and the Iron Age, deriving from the materials that prehistoric peoples had used to manufacture weapons and implements.

The first man to establish the Three-Age System was the Danish scholar Christian Thomsen (1788–1865). He had started life as an import-export merchant, but became interested in archaeology after rescuing a fine collection of old coins during the British bombardment of Copenhagen in 1807 and carrying it to safety to the Royal Cabinet of Antiquities. He became the unpaid secretary of the new National Museum in 1816, and originally he formulated the Three-Age System as a means of classifying the museum collections in a businesslike way. He reasoned that prehistory must have been divided into three ages in that order for the simple reason that people would not have used stone or wood or bone for their weapons and tools if bronze had been available, and that bronze was bound to have been superseded by the more efficient iron.

His successor at the Museum was Jens Jacob Worsaae (1821–85), who could claim to be the first truly professional archaeologist. He studied law, but as a schoolboy he had become intensively interested in antiquities through helping Thomsen at the Museum. Even though he quarrelled with Thomsen and had to apply direct to the King of Denmark for funds for archaeological research, he greatly extended Thomsen's basic theories and demonstrated the validity of the Three-Age System in field excavations and as a basis for prehistoric chronology all over the world. As early as 1843, when he was

Silbury Hill from the air. The Duke of Northumberland sank a shaft from top to bottom in 1776 but found no treasure.

still a young man of only 22, he had published a definitive book on Danish antiquities, *Danmarks Oldtid* (Prehistory of Denmark), and was expounding the scientific principles to be followed during excavations—the need to make accurate drawings and descriptions, the need to take infinite care in the recording and removing of any object of whatever nature, particularly pottery and bones. Nothing must be overlooked; everything was a potential source of information.

The pioneering Danish classification of the Three-Age System was considerably elaborated by later scholars, and each of the ages was subdivided for greater refinement of definition; for instance, the Stone Age, which stretches for thousands of years back into the past, was subdivided into Old, Middle, and New. *Palaeolithic* (itself divided into Lower, Middle, and Upper) is the technical term for the Old Stone Age, beginning with the emergence of man down to the end of the geological Ice Age; *Mesolithic* for the Middle Stone Age, the period of transition beginning in the early post-glacial period around 8300 BC; and *Neolithic* for the New Stone Age which was heralded by the beginnings of agriculture as opposed to nomadic hunting in south-west Asia around 6000 BC.

The Three-Age System has outgrown its usefulness now, because modern studies have shown how impossible it is to apply rigid classifications of this kind with any consistency. But it was a wonderfully illuminating concept at the time, for it showed the past as a logical progression of cultures, a logical evolution of man's skills and talents and knowledge. It gave the past a coherent framework, in which artifacts could be compared and classified through *typology* (the study of shapes), and the spread of human knowledge could be traced through *diffusionism* (the study of the spread of cultural traits from their point of origin). Ideas and concepts of this kind, as expounded by Worsaae, fitted admirably the new intellectual atmosphere of the nineteenth century, the new interest in science of every kind, the new preoccupation with man and all his works.

Previously, most thinking about the past had been conditioned and limited by theological concepts based on a literal belief in the

Skeletons in a Danish megalithic tomb. An illustration from the English edition of Worsaae's *Danmarks Oldtid* (published as *The Primeval Antiquities of Denmark*, 1849).

Biblical accounts of the origin of the world. In 1650, Archbishop James Ussher of Armagh, in Ireland, produced a timetable of world history based on *Genesis* and the Hebrew date for the Flood (2348 BC), which 'proved' that the Creation took place in the year 4004 BC. This date was further refined by Dr John Lightfoot, Vice-Chancellor of Cambridge University: 'Man was created by the Trinity on October 23, 4004 BC, at nine o'clock in the morning.'

But by the first years of the nineteenth century, geologists were beginning to realise, from their study of the rocks and soils that make up the crust of the earth, that the creation of the world had been a very much longer process. They had noted that rocks had formed in vast layers, or strata, one on top of the other, as a result of convulsive subterranean upheavals, and that the process of rock formation was still continuing. By studying these strata it was possible to work out a rough timetable of what came first—and the time-scale involved was unimaginably huge.

At the same time there was a growing interest in *palaeontology*, the study of extinct organisms, and it was becoming clear, however reluctantly, that Man himself was very much older than had been supposed. Human bones and man-made flint implements were found in unmistakable association with the bones of such extinct animals as woolly rhinoceros, mammoths, and cave lions, embedded in layers of rock. By the middle of the nineteenth century, European scientists were prepared to admit the great antiquity of Man, in theory at least.

Then in 1856, in a cave in the Neanderthal Valley near Dusseldorf in Germany, the bones were found of a man whose skull differed very considerably from a modern human skull. This was the first discovery of the celebrated Neanderthal Man, whose remains have since been found in many parts of the world. No one knew then how old this skull was, but the heavy brow-ridges and massive jaws suggested a creature that might be pre-Man. It is now recognised that Neanderthal Man lived from about 110,000 to 35,000 years ago; he was a skilful hunter, a good tool-maker, and could make fires, and buried his dead carefully with funerary offerings, suggesting a form of religion. He may have been a distinct species of Man, but some scholars think he was a direct ancestor of *homo sapiens*.

It was in this atmosphere of intellectual ferment that Charles Darwin, in 1859, published his theory of evolution in his book *On the Origin of Species by means of Natural Selection;* and this was closely followed in 1863 by T. H. Huxley's application of the evolution theory to Man himself in *Man's Place in Nature*. With these major events, the science of archaeology began to come into its own. It was now established that Man had a great antiquity, that prehistory stretched back for thousands of years into the remote past, and that this prehistory could be classified in a broad framework of the successive Ages of Stone, Bronze and Iron. It could be said that the main principles of archaeological study had been born, and archaeology was ready to embark upon its Heroic Age.

3

The Heroic Age of Archaeology

Sometimes the story of how a discovery was made is more fascinating than the discovery itself. The pioneers of archaeological excavation were often men of great personality and character whose exploits have become almost legendary. In the early days they were frankly treasure-hunters, archaeological freebooters who plundered sites ruthlessly for the objects of value they might contain. It was looting, not archaeology, and today we read of them with a horrified fascination.

GIOVANNI BATTISTA BELZONI

Belzoni was one of the earliest giants—in every sense of the term, for he was six feet seven inches tall. He was born in 1778 in Padua, in Italy, and was originally intended for a monastery, but instead he studied mechanical engineering and in 1803 he came to England, where he made a living as a strong-man in a circus under the billing of 'the Italian Giant'. In 1815 he made his way to Egypt, hoping to sell to the Turkish Sultan's viceroy an ingenious form of hydraulic pumping machine he had invented to give life to the desert again; but when this came to nothing, Belzoni turned to archaeology for a living. He worked as an agent for the British Consul General in Egypt, Henry Salt, who was an enthusiastic private collector of relics; but much of his brigandage was carried out on a freelance basis. His prodigious size and physical strength served him in good stead when he was forcing his way into ancient tombs or fighting off hostile Arabs—or the rival gangs of 'archaeologists' from other countries intent on pillage.

Medal struck by English friends of Belzoni, 1821, to commemorate his opening of the pyramid of Chephren at Giza in 1818

27

He described his adventures in 1820 in a book modestly entitled *Narrative of the Operations and Recent Discoveries within the Pyramids, Temples, Tombs, and Excavations, in Egypt and Nubia,* which gives a vivid picture of the dangers and discomforts involved in early Egyptian exploration, as well as the wholesale destruction that went on:

'Of some of these tombs many persons could not withstand the suffocating air, which often causes fainting . . . In some places there is not more than a vacancy of a foot left, which you must contrive to pass through in a creeping posture like a snail, on pointed and keen stones, that cut like glass. After getting through these passages, some of them two or three hundred yards long, you generally find a more commodious place, perhaps high enough to sit. But what a place of rest!—surrounded by bodies, by heaps of mummies in all directions; which, previous to my being accustomed to the sight, impressed me with horror . . . After the exertion of entering into such a place, through a passage of fifty, a hundred, three hundred, or perhaps six hundred yards, nearly overcome, I sought a resting place, found one and contrived to sit; but when my weight bore on the body of an Egyptian, it crushed it like a band-box. I naturally had recourse to my hands to sustain my weight, but they found no better support; so that I sunk altogether among the broken mummies, with a crash of bones, rags, and wooden cases, which raised such a dust as kept me motionless for a quarter of an hour, waiting till it subsided again. I could not remove from the place, however, without increasing it, and every step I took I crushed a mummy in some part or other . . . The purpose of my researches was to rob the Egyptians of their papyri; of which I found a few hidden in their breasts, under their arms, in the space above the knees, or on the legs, and covered by numerous folds of cloth, that envelop the mummy.'

And so Belzoni charged through the antiquities of Egypt, smashing down sealed doors of tombs with a battering ram, exploring, sketching, looting. In the Valley of the Kings at Luxor, he battered his way through the rock-choked galleries of the magnificent sepulchre of the Pharaoh Sethos I, the father of Ramesses the Great, and from it he removed the Pharaoh's superbly carved alabaster sarcophagus, which he triumphantly brought back to London and sold for £2,000—it is now on display in the Soane Museum.

Belzoni also organised the removal of other great monuments. He

Giovanni Battista
Belzoni, 'the Italian
Giant', in Turkish
dress.

G. BELZONI.

managed to remove a 22-foot obelisk from the island of Philae and
sail it down the Nile, and he outmanoeuvred a rival French gang to
gain possession of a huge bust of Ramesses II for Consul General
Salt (and, ultimately, the British Museum in London). He cleared an
entrance through the sand that completely buried the great carved
rock temples at Abu Simbel, which were recently saved from the
waters of the Aswan Dam by a mammoth UNESCO operation.

But perhaps his most notable achievement was to become the first man in modern times to enter and explore Chephren's pyramid at Giza, in 1818. He paid eighty Arab workmen two and a half pence each a day to dig through the sand that had engulfed the lower part of the pyramid, and an army of boys and girls he paid one and a half pence each a day to carry the spoil away; after sixteen days they found a chink between two stones on the north face of the pyramid. This proved to be the entrance to a passage that had been forced by earlier tomb-robbers in antiquity. This passage was too dangerous even for a man of Belzoni's reckless courage; undaunted, he started searching the facade again and found another way in down a narrow tunnel. At the end of it, he had to raise a block of granite that lay across the passage, until he finally managed to squeeze his huge frame through and into the main burial chamber of the king, Chephren, who had built the pyramid as a tomb for himself. But robbers had been there before him, some 2,000 years earlier, and all he found in the empty sarcophagus was a handful of cow-bones.

Belzoni died in December, 1823, in Nigeria; he had caught dysentery there, on his way to search for the city of Timbuktu. His epitaph in a recent Dictionary of Archaeology is crushingly terse: 'A picturesque and unprincipled collector of Egyptian antiques in 1817–19, who enriched European collections enormously, but by the worst possible methods, destroying in two years almost as much as time alone had done in two thousand.'

HEINRICH SCHLIEMANN

The story of Heinrich Schliemann and his discovery of Troy is one of the epic romances of archaeology. He was born in 1822 at the village of Neubuckow in what is now East Germany, the son of a Lutheran pastor much addicted to drink and heroic legends. At the age of eight, Heinrich was given as a Christmas present from his father an illustrated history book which had in it an engraving showing the ancient town of Troy in flames. Nothing then was known of Troy except as the setting for Homer's epics, but there and then young Schliemann vowed that one day he would find the lost city of Troy and excavate the mighty walls the artist had imagined for his engraving.

After school, at the age of fourteen, he started work as a grocer's assistant. But he never forgot his love of the legends of Troy, and he now set out to make sufficient money to be able, one day, to carry out his dream; or that, at least, was the story he liked to put around later in life. He became a businessman in the indigo trade, learned eight foreign languages in a single year in order to exploit foreign markets, made a fortune in Russia by the time he was thirty and made another fortune in California during the Gold Rush, and retired from business in his forties as a multi-millionaire. He learned Greek so as to be able to read Homer in the original, and in 1868 he set off for Greece:

> 'At last I was able to realise the dream of my life, and to visit at my leisure the country of the heroes whose adventures had delighted and comforted my childhood.'

Sophia Schliemann, wearing the jewellery her husband believed had belonged to Helen of Troy.

He went to Ithaca, the home of Odysseus, and on the summit of Aetos he impulsively started digging for the palace of Odysseus where his wife, Penelope, had kept the horde of suitors at bay. He found little except what seemed to be a small family graveyard, some urns containing human ashes; and with the romantic zeal that characterised all his deductions, he leapt to the conclusion that these were probably the ashes of Odysseus and Penelope.

But before he could settle down to his long-planned excavation of Troy, this lonely middle-aged man, whose first marriage had failed miserably, felt he needed a wife—a Greek girl-bride who would be his Helen of Troy and help him to live out in real life his Trojan fantasies. The Archbishop of Athens recommended a suitable candidate, a sixteen-year-old girl called Sophia Engastromenos who fulfilled the basic qualifications of being poor, pretty, and loving. He paid a secret visit to her school, listened to her declaiming Homer, quizzed her on the dates of the Roman Emperor Hadrian's visit to Athens, fell madly in love, and married her twenty days later.

And so in 1871 he came at last to Homer's 'windy plain of Troy' to start the first of his four campaigns. Schliemann had already decided that the site of Troy was a high mound or *tell* called Hissarlik overlooking the Dardanelles; it was here, he was convinced, that Homer's heroes had battled for ten long years.

With an army of eighty workmen he drove a great gash straight into the steep northern face of Hissarlik. Immediately he came across a bewildering tangle of ruined towns lying haphazardly on top of one another; there was not one ancient Troy, but several. Schliemann identified nine separate cities, but later scholars have identified no fewer than 57 layers of occupation. Schliemann, with his naively literal faith in Homer, was convinced that what he believed to be the real Troy, Homer's Troy (which most scholars of his day thought was merely a romantic fable), lay at the bottom of this pile. So he ruthlessly cut his way down, destroying everything in his path, until after two years of toil he came across a great mass of masonry with walls twenty feet high—sufficiently heroic in size, he felt, to have been those of the Great Tower of Priam's Troy.

And then on June 14, 1873, the day before the excavation was due to end, Schliemann found gold. He dismissed the workmen, and he and Sophia worked alone to unearth the treasure, an incredible hoard of 8,700 golden objects, including cups, vases, bracelets, rings, necklaces, and a magnificent golden diadem made up of 16,000

OPPOSITE
The Oseberg Ship in the Viking Ship Museum, Oslo.

separate pieces of gold. With tears in his eyes, Schliemann loaded his lovely young wife with the treasures: 'Darling,' he said, 'this is the most beautiful moment of our life; you are wearing the treasure of Helen of Troy!'

We know now (and Schliemann himself reluctantly was forced to admit it before his own death in 1890) that the Treasure of Priam, as he called it, had never adorned Helen of Troy. The ruined city in which the treasure was found had been almost at the bottom of the great mound of Hissarlik, at a level which archaeologists now call Troy II. It was very early indeed, somewhere around 2300 BC—a full thousand years before the Troy that had perished in the Trojan War around 1250 BC (Troy VIIA). In his enthusiasm and inexperience, Schliemann had driven his way straight through the Homeric city he was looking for.

His discovery caused a sensation. Schliemann broke his agreement with the Turkish government and smuggled the treasure to his house in Athens, and eventually he presented it to Germany in exchange for a string of honours. The collection was housed in the Ethnological Museum in Berlin, but at the outbreak of the Second World War it was divided up and hidden. The Treasure of Priam itself was deposited for safe keeping in a huge concrete bunker near Berlin Zoo, but when Berlin fell to the Russian army in 1945, the Treasure of Priam disappeared. Some think it was taken to Russia, others that it was melted down by looters; occasionally a piece of goldwork comes on the black market and is hailed as having come from the Schliemann collection, but no one now believes that the main body of the Treasure of Priam will ever be seen again.

Schliemann's instinct for buried gold took him next to Mycenae, Homer's Golden Mycenae, which had been the city of the victorious Greek commander in the Trojan War, Agamemnon. Mycenae then had been one of the most important city-states of Greece, surrounded by immense walls pierced by an imposing Lion Gate. It was to Mycenae that Agamemnon had returned in triumph after the fall of Troy, only to be murdered in his bath by his wife Clytemnestra and her lover. The glory of Mycenae had long since died, but the great walls remained, and the legend of tragedy and treasure.

Others had been to Mycenae in search of the legendary gold; but none had Schliemann's nose for it. Schliemann started digging just inside the Great Wall, making a trench 113 feet square, and immediately exposing a double circle of sculptured gravestones. Digging

'The mask of Agamemnon' found by Heinrich Schliemann at Mycenae.

33

Schliemann's excavation of the royal grave circle at Mycenae. In the foreground is Sophia Schliemann.

further in a fever of excitement, he found the first of the five celebrated shaft-graves of Mycenae. They varied in depth from three to fifteen feet. For 25 days Schliemann and Sophia worked in them alone, scraping away layer upon layer of soil with a penknife; and what they found during these 25 days has been described as 'one of the richest archaeological discoveries ever made.'

Inside the shaft-graves were the bodies of nineteen people—men, women, and two children. They were surrounded with numerous golden treasures of beautiful workmanship. Schliemann was convinced he had found the graves of Homer's Mycenean royal family, the graves of murdered Agamemnon and his companions. In the fifth grave he met his ultimate moment of fulfilment. There were three male bodies in it, with golden breastplates and magnificent golden face-masks. When the first two masks were raised, the skulls beneath them crumbled away at once. But the third was different:

'Of the third body, which lay at the north end of the tomb, the round face, with all its flesh, had been wonderfully preserved

under its ponderous golden mask. There was no vestige of hair, but both eyes were perfectly visible, also the mouth, which, owing to the enormous weight that had been pressed down upon it, was wide open and showed thirty-two beautiful teeth.'

Schliemann lifted the golden mask and kissed it. And that night he sent to the King of Greece perhaps the most famous telegram in the history of archaeology: 'Today I have gazed upon the face of Agamemnon.'

Yet Schliemann's impulsive romanticism had led him astray once again. The golden masks were not those of Agamemnon and his men, but of princes who had died some four hundred years earlier. For the great Mycenean civilisation that Schliemann had uncovered had flourished for a full six centuries before Agamemnon led his confederation of bronze-clad warriors against Troy.

Schliemann's blind belief in the literal truth of the classical writers led him to make many such blunders of interpretation. But it was this faith that led him to attempt a search that most scholars dismissed as a waste of time; and in the course of that search, Schliemann was responsible for uncovering a brilliant Bronze Age civilisation that no one had suspected existed. Indeed, if he had not been quite so much of a businessman, he would have discovered the unsuspected Minoan civilisation of Crete as well—Schliemann tried to buy the land containing the ancient site of Knossos but broke off the negotiations when he discovered he was being cheated over the number of olive trees involved, and it was left to a later archaeologist, Sir Arthur Evans, to reveal the lost glory of yet another pre-Homeric civilisation in the Aegean.

SIR AUSTEN HENRY LAYARD

At about the same time as the young Heinrich Schliemann was dreaming of Troy, a small boy in England was dreaming of the Orient, inspired by *The Arabian Nights* and Sir Walter Scott's romances of the East. His name was Austen Henry Layard, later to become famous as 'the father of Assyriology'.

'To them I attribute that love of travel and adventure which took me to the East, and led me to the discovery of the ruins of Nineveh.'

Nineveh: the name conjures up powerful images of the warlike Assyrians of the Bible. It was the capital of the Assyrian Empire from the eighth century BC until it was destroyed by the Medes in 612 BC. It had been the capital of the terrible Sennacherib, who was eventually murdered by his own sons: 'Woe to the bloody city!' the prophet Nahum had cried. 'The noise of the whip, and the noise of the rattling wheels, and the prancing horses, and the jumping chariots . . .'

But where had Nineveh been? After its destruction by the Medes, it disappeared. Some 2,000 years ago, the Roman poet Lucian wrote, 'As for Nineveh, it is already gone, and there is no trace of it left.' By the middle of the nineteenth century, awakening antiquarian interest had placed it somewhere in Iraq near the modern town of Mosul on the River Tigris.

Layard happened to be at the right place at the right time when Assyrian archaeology began, spectacularly, in the 1840s. He himself was not an archaeologist. He had studied law, but at heart he was an

Hound with attendant. Detail from a relief in the North Palace of Ashurbanipal at Nineveh

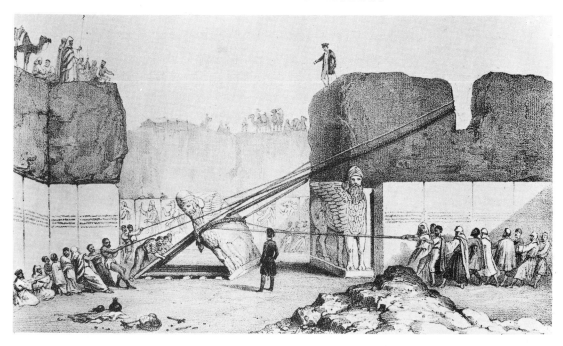

Removing the human-headed winged lions from Ashurnasirpal II's palace at Nimrud for shipment to the British Museum in 1848.

adventurer, a restless young man who could not stand the confines of a lawyer's office and threw it up in order to go travelling overland to Ceylon, where he planned to become a tea-planter. It was while Layard was in Constantinople that news came that the French vice-consul at Mosul, Paul-Emile Botta, had made a momentous discovery of an ancient Assyrian palace under a great mound—and it was probably Nineveh. He had started digging into the mound of Kuyunjik, near Mosul, but when nothing turned up for several weeks, he turned his attention to the mound at Khorsabad, a few miles further north, where workmen were said to have found some sculptured stones. Success was immediate, and Botta started unearthing great quantities of huge limestone slabs covered with powerful relief carvings of Assyrian armies in action. Later studies proved that the Khorsabad site was not Nineveh, as Botta had thought, but the city of Dur-Sharrukin, or Fort of Sargon, which had been built in 717 BC by Sargon II, King of Assyria from 721–705 BC.

Layard's sense of adventure was fired at once. From the British Ambassador at Constantinople, Sir Stratford Canning, he begged a grant of £60 to do some digging for Britain. Then:

'I crossed the mountains of Pontus and the great steppes of the Usun Yilak as fast as post-horses could carry me, descended the

37

high lands into the valley of the Tigris, galloped over the vast plains of Assyria, and reached Mosul in twelve days.'

After this flamboyant start, Layard's archaeological career only lasted for less than a decade. But in these few years he made some spectacular discoveries, and many of the most striking Assyrian monuments in the British Museum today were hustled out of Mesopotamia by him. He started by digging into the mound of Nimrud, named after the Biblical Nimrod, that 'mighty hunter before the Lord'. Layard attacked it with spirited enthusiasm and with a small band of workmen as untrained in archaeological techniques as himself. And by the end of the first day, he had uncovered traces of two different Assyrian palaces. There were colossal figures of winged human-headed lions and bulls, immense stone-lined chambers and galleries covered with inscriptions and sculptured reliefs of Assyrian warriors:

'Two chariots, drawn by horses richly caparisoned, were each occupied by three warriors, the principal was clothed in a complete set of mail . . . The left hand, the arm being fully extended, grasped a bow at full stretch . . . A second warrior urged three

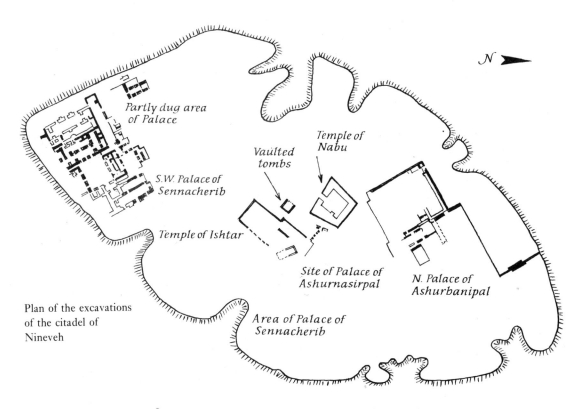

Plan of the excavations of the citadel of Nineveh

horses, which were galloping across the plains. Under the horses' feet, and scattered about the relief, were the conquered, wounded by the arrows of the conquerors.'

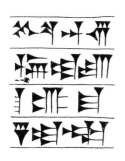

Cuneiform script

The massive human-headed bulls, each weighing ten tons of black shining basalt, were uprooted with crowbars and dragged on rollers across the blazing desert for shipment to the British Museum via Bombay. So were hundreds of carvings and reliefs, and thousands of inscriptions in a cuneiform (wedge-shaped) writing that scholars were still not able to decipher properly. It was as a result of this ignorance of the language that Layard at first thought that Nimrud was Nineveh; in fact, his best-selling book on his discoveries, which he published in 1849, was called *Nineveh and its Remains*. It was only later, when the cuneiform inscriptions had been deciphered, that it emerged that Nimrud was actually the Biblical city of Calah, and contained palaces built first by Shalmaneser I (1274-45 BC) and then by Ashurnasirpal II (883-859 BC). Like Nineveh, Calah too had been destroyed in 612 BC when the Medes overthrew the Assyrian empire.

But Layard was, in fact, destined to discover Nineveh itself. After exploring Nimrud, he moved to the mound of Kuyunjik, near Mosul, that the Frenchman Paul-Emile Botta had abandoned earlier. Once again, Layard was lucky; only a few inches lower than the level at which Botta had given up, Layard struck the walls of one of the greatest palaces of Nineveh, the palace of Sennacherib:

'I opened no less than seventy-one halls, chambers and passages whose walls, almost without exception, had been panelled with slabs of sculptured alabaster recording the wars, the triumphs, and the great deeds of the Assyrian king. By a rough calculation about 9,880 feet, or nearly two miles, of bas-reliefs, with twenty-seven portals formed by colossal winged bulls and lion-sphinxes, were uncovered in that part of the building explored by my researches.'

And most of these, as well as the celebrated Black Obelisk of Shalmaneser III from Nimrud, went off on the long trail to London.

From Sennacherib's palace he also recovered a great library of clay tablets covered with cuneiform writing—some 26,000 of them piled up in two large chambers. In 1854, soon after Layard returned to London to start a career in the diplomatic service, his former assistant found the royal library that Sennacherib's grandson,

Ashurbanipal (668–627 BC), our 'earliest conservationist', had built up. The way that this library came to London rather than to Paris is a reflection of the intense nationalistic rivalry that existed in nineteenth-century archaeology. After Botta had abandoned the mound at Kuyunjik, the French had retained certain rights there; but when the palace of Sennacherib had been revealed, the British were curious to know what might lie under the French section, so they made a moonlight raid on it. At the first stroke of the spade, the palace of Ashurbanipal began to emerge . . .

LORD ELGIN

The Elgin Marbles in the British Museum are perhaps the most notorious example of looting in the name of national prestige in the history of archaeology; and this, too, came about largely as a result of intense rivalry with the French.

Thomas Bruce, seventh Earl of Elgin, was born in Scotland in 1766, descended from the family of Scotland's great warrior-hero, King Robert the Bruce. Like other young men of the aristocracy in that age, he made his career in a mixture of the army, politics, and the diplomatic service. He was appointed British Envoy Extraordinary at Berlin at the age of 25, and then in 1799, at the age of 32, he was made Ambassador Extraordinary to the Sublime Porte Selim III, Sultan of Turkey, in Constantinople.

Greece was then under Turkish rule, and it was suggested to Lord Elgin that he could make his embassy to Constantinople 'beneficial to the progress of the Fine Arts in Great Britain' if he brought back drawings and casts of classical Greek sculpture and architecture from Athens.

Amiably, Lord Elgin agreed, and recruited a team of artists and craftsmen which he sent to Athens to start on the work of drawing and modelling what was left of the classical temples of the Acropolis.

The crowning glory of the Acropolis, the Parthenon, had been built during the time of Pericles in the fifth century BC as a vast temple to the goddess Athena. It was made of glowing marble from Mount Pentelicus, a masterpiece of subtly curved lines to create the illusion of straightness. Inside the temple stood a colossal forty-foot statue of Athena made of gold and ivory, created by the leading Athenian sculptor of his day, Pheidias. But it was the decorative scheme for the Parthenon itself that was his greatest achievement.

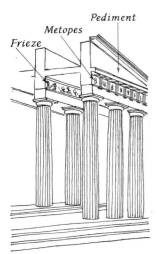

Pediment
Metopes
Frieze

Diagram of the Parthenon showing the position of the Elgin Marbles

The Elgin Marbles: horsemen preparing for the Panathenaic Procession.

Each gable-end was crowned by a triangular, 100-foot pediment crowded with brightly painted statues grouped in tableaux. Below the pediments, and stretching all the way round the outer colonnades, were a series of carved marble panels called metopes, each four feet square, 92 in all, depicting scenes from classical mythology. And all the way round the top of the inner walls of the temple, almost hidden by the outer colonnade, there was a continuous frieze which represented in vivid carving the great ceremonial procession that was held in Athens every fourth year to celebrate the Panathenaic Festival. The frieze of this crowded procession, winding its way up the Acropolis, was nearly 600 feet long in all.

In 1687 the Parthenon was severely damaged when the Turks were besieged on the Acropolis by an invading Venetian army. The Parthenon was being used as a gunpowder magazine; a cannonball scored a direct hit on the magazine, and the whole building exploded, tearing huge gaps in the colonnades on both sides and destroying much of the statuary. The victorious Venetian general tried to carry off some of the rest to celebrate his victory, but as he was attempting to lower some statues from the western pediment the tackle broke and the whole group fell to the ground and was shattered. One of his officers managed to remove two heads from one of the metopes, however—the heads of a centaur and a Lapith, which are now in the National Museum in Copenhagen.

By the end of the eighteenth century Athens was a dingy little town of no more than a thousand houses, with a Turkish garrison living on the Acropolis itself. The temples were in desolate condition, and the statues were in constant danger of further damage.

Lord Elgin's original intention was simply to draw and measure and record. But by the time permission was eventually obtained from the Turkish authorities to do this, the idea of actually removing some of the pieces had crept in; Lord Elgin's cultural crusade for the 'progress of the Fine Arts in Great Britain' had altered drastically. Soon the first of the metopes were being detached from the walls of the Parthenon and taken down to Piraeus for shipment to England: the collection of the Elgin Marbles had begun.

'I should wish,' wrote Lord Elgin, 'to have, of the Acropolis, examples in the actual object of each thing, and architectural ornament—of each cornice, each frieze, each capital—of the decorated ceilings, of the fluted columns, specimens of the different architectural orders—of metopes and the like, as much as possible. Finally everything in the way of sculpture, medals and curious marbles that can be discovered by assiduous and indefatigable excavation.'

To get at some of the sculptures, Elgin's men had to destroy parts of the fabric of the temple. But they also excavated the rubble at the bottom of the walls, where fragments had been allowed to lie unheeded by the Turks, and in this way they rescued some fine pieces from the pediments.

Not content with the Parthenon, however, and under pressure from the Turkish authorities to allow the French a share of the loot, Elgin stripped what he could from the other temples, including one of the delicate sculptured Caryatid columns from the tiny Erechtheum temple. His agents sent back to London crate after crate of statuary. One shipload of marbles suffered disaster on the way: the *Mentor* sank in the Mediterranean with seventeen crates on board, and it cost Lord Elgin £5,000 to salvage them and bring them safely to England.

In this picture of the first temporary Elgin Room at the British Museum in 1819, the seated figures in the foreground are Sir Benjamin West, the artist and a member of the Select Committee, and Sir Joseph Planta, Principal Librarian of the Museum. In the right foreground is the artist of the painting, A. Archer.

In 1803 Lord Elgin's tour of duty ended, and he was looking forward to a hero's return to London. But while making his leisurely way home across the Continent, war broke out between Britain and France. Lord Elgin and his wife were arrested as prisoners of war.

It was to be three years before Lord Elgin was paroled and allowed to return home. By then his wife, who had been released earlier, had left him for another man. And the priceless Marbles still lay unheeded in their packing cases.

Lord Elgin quickly arranged to put them on display, in June, 1807. The effect on the artistic world was electrifying at first, but gradually public opinion began to change. Lord Elgin had been financially ruined by his enormous expenditure in Constantinople and Athens, and now he tried to sell the collection to the Government for what it had cost him, which he reckoned at £62,440. The Government refused. Five years later he tried again, this time asking for £74,000 to cover the mounting interest charges on the money he had already spent. Parliament responded by setting up a Select Committee to examine the whole controversy, for Lord Elgin was now being assailed on all sides for 'plundering' the Parthenon.

In the event, the Select Committee vindicated all his actions; but the price they put on the collection was only £35,000, which Lord Elgin had no alternative but to accept. In 1816, the Elgin Marbles were transferred to the ownership of the British Museum, where they can now be seen displayed to splendid effect in the specially designed Duveen Gallery.

Lord Elgin died in 1841, ruined, disillusioned, and derided. To the end he protested that what he had done was 'wholly for the purpose of securing to Great Britain and through it to Europe in general, the most effectual public knowledge, and means of improving, by the excellence of Grecian art in sculpture.'

Certainly he had saved the Marbles from further damage—the fragments that are still left on the buildings are in terrible condition now. And he had succeeded in awakening aesthetic appreciation in England to the glories of classical art. But he had done it at bitter cost to himself.

JEAN-FRANÇOIS CHAMPOLLION

Jean-François Champollion was not an archaeological excavator. Yet his is one of the most celebrated names in the history of archaeology, for he was the scholar who deciphered the ancient Egyptian hieroglyphic writing on the Rosetta Stone and thus opened the way to modern Egyptology.

When Napoleon Bonaparte invaded Egypt in 1798, he took with him a group of over a hundred distinguished French scholars whose task was to survey the country and its monuments and remove anything worth removing for the greater glory of France. In August, 1799, a French officer called Pierre Bouchard who was in charge of a detachment of troops working on the fortifications of a place called Rosetta on the western side of the Nile Delta, noticed a slab of old black basalt which had been built into the wall of an Arab fort that was being demolished. He saw that it was covered with inscriptions of three different kinds, and he guessed they might be three different versions of the same text. One of the languages was Greek; but the other two scripts were forms of the ancient Egyptian language that no one could decipher at the time—*demotic* (a popular cursive script) and *hieroglyphic* (picture-writing, literally 'sacred carved signs').

Copies of all the texts were made and circulated amongst the scholars of Europe. The Rosetta Stone itself was destined for the

The Rosetta Stone.

Louvre, but after Napoleon's defeat in Egypt in 1801 it was appropriated by the British with the help of a detachment of artillerymen and despatched to the British Museum instead: 'A most valuable relick of antiquity,' wrote the man who captured it, Major-General Sir Tomkyns Turner, 'the feeble but only yet discovered link of the Egyptian to the known languages, a proud trophy of the arms of Britain (I could almost say *spolia opima*), not plundered from defenceless inhabitants, but honourably acquired by the fortune of war.'

One of the scholars who took a particular interest in the inscriptions was a young Frenchman called Jean-François Champollion. He had been a brilliant and precocious schoolboy with a passion for old languages, so much so that by the time he was eighteen he had taught himself Arabic, Syriac, Hebrew, Latin, Greek, and the medieval form of ancient Egyptian called Coptic. Like Layard and Schliemann, he had been fired in his childhood with romantic visions of the past—the antiquities of Egypt. He was only nine years old when the Rosetta Stone was discovered, but from 1802 he determined to equip himself with sufficient ancient languages to be able one day to decipher it.

He first saw a plaster cast of the Stone in Paris in 1808, when he was eighteen years old. By then he was already engaged on writing a monumental history of *Egypt under the Pharaohs*. It would take fourteen years before he succeeded in deciphering the Stone and breaking the hieroglyphic script. In 1822 he announced his first successes in a letter to the secretary of the Academy of Inscriptions in Paris, entitled *Letter to Monsieur Dacier in Regard to the Alphabet of the Phonetic Hieroglyphs*.

Hieroglyphs in the cartouche of Tutankhamun

It should be remembered that this was a period of great scholarly excitement and controversy over ancient languages. The cuneiform (wedge-shaped) writings of the ancient kingdoms of Mesopotamia had still not yet been deciphered. Everybody had a theory, everybody had a system, for tackling these enigmatic symbols that were emerging from the sands of the East.

The scholars who worked on the Rosetta Stone had one great advantage; the text was bilingual, and because one of the languages was Greek they knew what the inscription meant (it was the copy of an honorific decree of Ptolemy V in 196 BC). Egyptian hieroglyphs had always been assumed to be secret religious symbols known only to the long-dead priests of Egypt—even Champollion himself started with that assumption. But an English scholar, Dr Thomas

Young, provided some important clues that helped Champollion; he noted how some of the hieroglyphs were enclosed in oval framings, called *cartouches*, as if to emphasise a symbol or name of special importance, and he tentatively identified some outstanding names in the Greek text like Ptolemy with individual cartouches. It was the first indication that the hieroglyphs were in part alphabetic.

Champollion was able to proceed from there, by working out phonetic equivalents of other hieroglyphs until a full alphabet emerged. But the language itself was still unknown; the alphabet merely enabled one to read the names, it gave no hint of the grammar or structure of the language. Champollion found the key, by confirming the kinship of the language of the hieroglyphs to Coptic.

Champollion had been studying Coptic for years, building up a huge dictionary of words and learning to write and even speak it. It was a dead language by then; it only survived in the liturgy of the Coptic Church—the minority Christian church that represented the descendants of Christianised Egyptians whom the Arabs had conquered in the seventh century AD. Coptic was the last phase of the ancient Egyptian language, and was written in the Greek script with a few extra letters derived from hieroglyphs to represent sounds which could not be expressed in Greek.

The task of Champollion was immensely complicated, for it was much more than simply finding a symbol to fit each letter of the alphabet as we know it. There were three classes of symbols, in fact—*pictograms* (which represented whole words in picture form), *phonograms* (which represented the sounds of words), and *determinatives* (which determined the class of word spelled by the phonograms). In spite of the overwhelming evidence in support of his explanation, for the rest of his life, until he died of a stroke in 1832 at the early age of 42, he was subjected to constant criticism from resentful and jealous academics. It was not until more than thirty years after his death, when another bilingual stone was found in Egypt (the Decree of Canopus) and translated successfully according to Champollion's principles, that Champollion was finally vindicated.

EDWARD THOMPSON

Most of the spectacular enterprises of the Heroic Age of archaeology took place in Europe and the Near East. But the New World had its flamboyant adventurers, too. One such was the man who became known as Edouardo Thompson. He devoted his energies to finding the lost cities of the Maya civilisation in Central America, and in particular the so-called Sacred Well of the Dead at Chichén Itzá.

More than a thousand years ago, the Maya had built their ceremonial temple centres in the heart of the dense tropical forests of the Yucatan peninsula of Mexico; and chief amongst them was Chichén Itzá. While Europe was still in its Dark Ages, the Maya were a cultured and sophisticated people, deeply concerned with the problems of time and eternity, ruled by a priestly caste who knew the secrets of writing and mathematics and advanced astronomy. Their hieroglyphic script is still only partly deciphered; but we know that in their classic period they studied philosophy and practised all the arts, they developed a calendar that was more accurate than the Julian calendar in use in Europe at the time, they cultivated their crops and traded with their neighbours, and they built great temples on top of pyramids in which they carried out elaborate rites—including ritual human sacrifice to appease their gods.

Chichén Itzá was one of the main centres for this ritual. From the Great Plaza a 900-foot causeway led to the Sacred Well, or Cenote, a vast natural water-hole 180 feet in diameter formed by the caving-in of the thin limestone crust that covers the Yucatan peninsula. The water surface, green and slimy, lies seventy feet down the sheer walls of the Cenote; and it was into this sinister well that the Mayan priests would throw living people, men and women and even children, as well as treasure and votive offerings of all kinds.

When the Spanish Conquistadores overran the Yucatan in the sixteenth century, even they professed themselves appalled by the vestiges they encountered of this cult. For reasons which are not yet fully understood, the Mayan culture had collapsed and degenerated before the Spanish conquest, but the customs lingered on, as a missionary Spanish bishop, Diego de Landa, reported:

OPPOSITE
Above The Parthenon in about 1803, when the metopes were being removed by Lord Elgin's workmen. *Below* Fresco panel with bull-leaping scene from Knossos.

'Into this Well they have had and still have the custom of throwing men alive as a sacrifice to their gods in time of drought, and they believed that they would not die, though they never saw them again. They also threw in many other things like precious stones and things they prized . . .'

Bishop Landa collected much useful information about other customs and traditions, as well as burning old hieroglyphic books in

Chichén Itzá: the
Temple of the
Warriors, with the pair
of Feathered Serpent
columns that flank the
entrance.

an attempt to stamp out barbarism. But his lurid accounts of sacrificed virgins were forgotten until the nineteenth century, and the temples were engulfed in tropical vegetation.

In 1839 an American lawyer and diplomat called John Lloyd Stephens travelled into the interior of the Yucatan with the English topographical artist Frederick Catherwood. Victorian society was fascinated by the travellers' tales they brought back:

> 'Architecture, sculpture and painting, all the arts which embellish life, had flourished in this overgrown forest; orators, warriors and statesmen, beauty, ambition and glory had lived and passed away . . .'

Catherwood's powerful drawings evoked all the dark majesty of these overgrown ruins and appealed strongly to the Victorian taste for Gothic romance: the great plumed serpents and brutal monster-gods, the Temple of the Warriors, the ruined Court of a Thousand Columns, the huge Ball Court where warriors had played a strange game—a cross between net-ball and American football in which the losers forfeited their lives.

At the end of the nineteenth century another English traveller, Alfred Maudslay, penetrated the hinterland of Mayan Mexico, this time bringing back a photographic record.

All these accounts fired the imagination of a New Englander called Edward Herbert Thompson. At first he was persuaded that the Maya were survivors of the legendary continent of Atlantis, which was said by Plato to have sunk without trace many centuries earlier; Thompson even wrote an enthusiastic college article to this effect, called *Atlantis not a Myth*.

When he got to the Yucatan, however, the old lust for treasure asserted itself, and he decided to explore the Well at Chichén Itzá to see if the presence of valuables in the water would prove the old tales of human sacrifice. Supported by archaeological enthusiasts in Massachusetts, he bought an old hacienda near the Well and imported an ancient clam-shaped grab with which to dredge up the alleged treasure from the accumulated mud at the bottom.

Gold cup and saucer
and gold bell from the
Cenote at Chichén Itzá

For three years, from 1904 to 1907, he laboured away at this task. Manipulated only by hand-lines held by local peasants, the grab would be manoeuvred out over the water and dropped below the surface, where it would claw up a pile of foul-smelling mud and slime and deposit it at the well-side. There Thompson and his helpers would sift through it carefully. For several weeks nothing

turned up except occasional animal skeletons and tree stumps. But eventually Thompson's patience was rewarded, and this crude contraption began to bring up, first, balls of aromatic copal resin, which early reports had said was burned during the sacrificial ceremony; then human bones and artifacts—wooden throwing-sticks, rubber objects, vessels of various kinds, arrowheads, copper chisels—and then a growing quantity of treasure: bracelets of bronze, necklaces of jade, statuettes, rings, ornaments of every kind, little bells of bronze or gold whose clapper had been removed.

In a flush of enthusiasm, Thompson roundly claimed the skeletons to be those of beautiful young virgins, although this would be difficult to prove from a study of the bones alone. Most of the skeletons, in fact, proved to be those of children, or old men and women.

Such was his zeal that Thompson even took lessons in deep-sea diving, and when the scoop had dug down to rock bottom, he went down in an old diving-suit through the inky water to search the crevices by hand; and it was now that he made his most spectacular discoveries, including two fine golden tiaras in the form of feathered serpents. It was hazardous work, but the results were rewarding enough; Thompson's friend, T. Willard, quoted Thompson as follows:

'The golden objects brought up, if simply thrown into the goldsmith's melting pot, would net several hundreds of thousands of dollars in bullion—dividend enough, if one were sufficiently sordid in mind, to justify all my investment of time, effort, and money in the undertaking.'

Thompson himself told a different version in his best-selling book, *People of the Serpent:* the value of the objects recovered from the Well was insignificant, he claimed—no doubt because he had by then abused his position as a United States consul to send all the treasure home in the diplomatic bag and present it to the Peabody Museum at Harvard, which had sponsored his exploration. The Mexican government, naturally enough, was furious and in 1959, after many years of diplomatic pressure, Harvard quietly returned some of the gold objects, although retaining the bulk of the collection.

Thompson's treachery made a sour ending to an adventurous enterprise. He had undoubtedly found the proof he was seeking, and the ornaments and little ankle-bells were ample evidence of the

An artist's archaeological reconstruction of the Mayan city of Chichén Itzá, showing the causeway from the great Plaza to the Cenote, or Sacred Well.

macabre rituals that had been enacted at the Well. His discoveries fired others, and the Carnegie Institute of Washington has spent a great deal of money excavating and restoring the ruins of Chichén Itzá and turning them into a popular tourist attraction. In 1961–2, and again in 1967, the Sacred Well was investigated by archaeologists using sophisticated scientific aids to purify the water to allow divers to see what they were doing; as a result, a further 2,600 finds were recovered to add to our knowledge of one of the most remarkable civilisations the world has known.

Jade Mayan carving
from Chichén Itzá

4

Archaeology
Comes of Age

THE FIRST DATING TECHNIQUES

The twentieth century has seen archaeology develop from an amateur and often bungling enthusiasm into a scientific profession which requires a high degree of training. But the foundations were being laid in the nineteenth century. While public attention was focused on those excavators who were primarily concerned with extracting finds from the ground for display in national museums, other scholars were unobtrusively trying to establish methods and techniques that would allow the finds to be interpreted and understood more clearly.

The Danish scholars, Thomsen and Worsaae, had already established the evolutionary Three-Age System to differentiate the technological stages of Man's development. But there was no proper time-scale for prehistory; no dates as such; no calendar, no chronology.

It was another Scandinavian, the Swedish scholar Oscar Montelius (1843–1921), who made the first significant steps in the development of a prehistoric calendar for Europe. After travelling widely throughout Europe, he constructed a series of relative timetables for each region, and then tried to join them all up into one absolute chronology. This technique is called *cross-dating*. He subdivided the Three Ages into smaller, numbered periods, and gave them absolute dates by cross-dating them right back to the known calendar dates of Egypt. It involved an extension of the technique of *typology* pioneered by Worsaae—the arrangement and classification of objects into significant types which reveal progressive development or degeneration. Montelius related the artifacts of a prehistoric, non-literate people with the artifacts of a people whose dates were known from their writings, such as the Greeks or the Egyptians.

The classic example that archaeologists are fond of quoting to illustrate the principle of typology is the motor-car: everyone can tell a vintage car from a modern car, and one can easily trace and date the development of cars from the original horseless carriage to the streamlined machines of today. One can also trace the effect of influences from other areas, such as the American car industry, and one can see how cars have been developed or improved to suit changing tastes and fashions and requirements.

Much the same kind of typological analysis can be applied to the development of pottery, or bronze axes, or ornamentation, or flint knives. Things change slowly, on the whole, and the trained archaeologist can learn to recognise characteristics of style and manufacture, to identify alien influences and borrowings, and then, by comparison with other known types, to deduce relationships. To take an example: when the Romans started expanding their rule northwards into Gaul and Germania during the first century BC, they came into contact with the Celts who lived there. The Celts by the fifth century BC had had a recognisable culture of their own; and they had also had trading contacts with the Greeks of the Mediterranean, so that some of their artifacts showed signs of Greek influence. After the Roman invasion of their countries they became increasingly Romanised and learned new fashions of manufacture, so one can reasonably assume that anything Romanised found in a Celtic grave should be dated *after* this historically authenticated contact had been made. This also helps to give, by association, a rough dating for any other objects that might be found in the same grave, although the objects could have been much older if they had been family heirlooms, for instance.

In this way, a chronology of prehistory gradually began to be built up, not always accurate in every particular but becoming clearer and clearer as more discoveries were made. What also became obvious was that the Three Ages had occurred at very different times in different parts of the world. The Bronze Age, for instance, seems to have moved across Europe like the sun, from east to west, reaching Britain around 2000 BC; whereas in Central and South America the Maya were still in their Bronze Age and the Incas had not yet discovered the principle of the wheel by the time the Spanish invaders arrived in the sixteenth century. The North American Indians and the Eskimos were still basically in their Stone Age culture when the first Europeans came on their scene.

GENERAL PITT RIVERS

One of the most important ways in which dating was further refined was through the development of *stratigraphy*, the technique of identifying different strata, or layers, of human activity on a site, just as a geologist differentiates strata of rock formations. It was pioneered by a man whom Sir Mortimer Wheeler has called 'the greatest of all archaeological excavators', General Augustus Lane-Fox Pitt Rivers. Remarkably enough, Pitt Rivers was not a

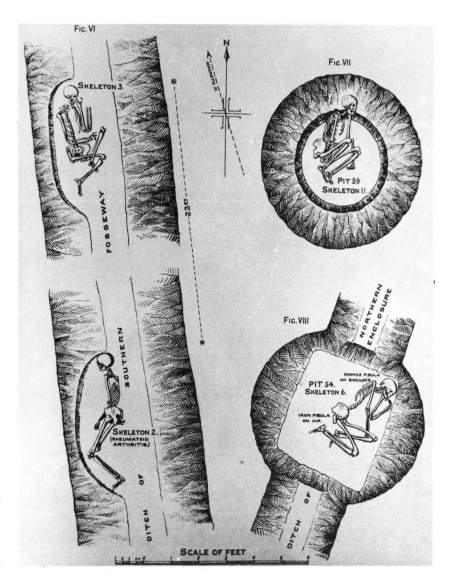

An illustration from *Excavations in Cranborne Chase* by General Pitt Rivers. Skeletons found in a Romano-British village at Rotherley are shown, with every relevant detail faithfully recorded.

professional archaeologist at all; he was a soldier who had only dabbled in archaeology before he came into an unexpected inheritance that changed his life.

In 1880, Pitt Rivers inherited large estates in Cranborne Chase in Dorset, and from then on he devoted all his time and means to a series of excavations of the villages round about. His four-volumed account, *Excavations in Cranborne Chase*, was published at his own expense between 1887 and 1898, and is regarded as an archaeological classic, combining meticulous observation and reporting with the rapid and detailed publication of all the finds that Schliemann had favoured. Pitt Rivers had the time, money, and staff to do more or less what he liked; but instead of pursuing treasure, he devoted himself to the exploration of the history of his own area, excavating the Iron Age villages of the British tribesmen and their Roman conquerors, the burial mounds of the Bronze Age and whatever Stone Age remains were available.

In its simplest form, the idea of archaeological stratification is based on the fact that in any one site where there has been human occupation over a long period, successive generations of settlement will be represented as superimposed layers of soil-disturbance, with the oldest layer at the bottom; and this 'story' can be read in cross-section when a trench is dug through it. These strata, or levels, can be composed of all kinds of things. Nearest the surface there may be the shadows of old plough-marks where the soil was tilled after the site had been abandoned and become overgrown. There may be stone foundations of buildings, 'ghost-walls' or 'robber-trenches' where walls used to be, trodden earthen floors, garbage-heaps, layers of ash where a building burned, and so on. Sometimes one can read intrusions through the layers—the clearing of accumulated debris to lay new foundations, the discoloration caused by digging holes to support wooden posts, the sinking of graves, even the removal of deep-rooted trees or burrowing by rabbits. All this multifarious evidence of activity shows up as bands of material of different colours and textures in the soil, studded with discarded objects and broken artifacts such as pottery, and the archaeologist has to be able to read it like a book. He must learn to recognise different deposits caused by different activities and to interpret how they came about; and he must also be able to record everything in detailed diagrammatic form so that other archaeologists will be able to assess for themselves the evidence on which he based his deductions.

SIR ARTHUR EVANS

Minoan pottery

Pitt Rivers died just as another English archaeologist was starting work on what was to become one of the most celebrated sites in Europe: the great Minoan palace of Knossos, in Crete. He was Sir Arthur Evans, the son of a wealthy Victorian businessman with a keen interest in scholarship and antiquities. Born in 1851, Arthur Evans inherited his father's passion for collecting, but he had a taste for travel and adventure, and for some of his youth was embroiled in the political struggles of the Balkans as a part-time foreign correspondent. At the age of 33 his bent for scholarship reasserted itself and he was appointed Keeper of the Ashmolean Museum in Oxford. He travelled to Greece and met Heinrich Schliemann; but Evans was interested in Schliemann's discoveries at Mycenae for 'non-Homeric' reasons—he was fascinated by the problem of the origins of Mycenean art. Where had its distinctive style come from? It was not classical Hellenic. Nor was it strictly Oriental, or strictly Egyptian, although there were tantalising echoes of all three. In addition, there was a clue that pointed in a completely new direction, towards Crete—minute engravings and markings on Mycenean gems that looked like hieroglyphic symbols also appeared on tiny seal-stones from Crete. Evans, who was extremely short-sighted, had microscopic sight at close range, and he could see these miniature markings better than anyone had done before.

Minoan bathtub
decorated with
dolphins

In 1899 Evans started digging in Crete at the site that Schliemann had earlier refused to buy. He was convinced that he would find there evidence of a pre-Homeric golden age of the Aegean, and he hoped that in the huge mound of Kephala, the traditional site of the palace of Knossos, he would come across enough examples of this non-Egyptian hieroglyphic writing to be able to decipher it. Almost at once he came across a huge labyrinth of buildings which he could recognise as being at least as old as the Mycenean civilisation, if not older. He had, in fact, stumbled on a whole new civilisation, which he named 'Minoan' after the King Minos of legend. It was Minos who had kept the monstrous Minotaur, half-man and half-bull, penned in a labyrinth below his palace and sacrificed to it every year twelve youths and maidens sent from Athens as tribute—until one year Theseus came as one of the hostages, slew the Minotaur in its lair and made his escape from the labyrinth by means of a clue of thread given to him by King Minos's lovestruck daughter, Ariadne.

The throne room in the palace at Knossos. The frescoes on the walls are modern restorations.

Minoan gold pendant

Evans was to devote the rest of his life and his considerable private fortune of £250,000 to the excavation and restoration of the palace of Knossos and the study of this newly-found prehistoric civilisation of the Aegean. By cross-dating with Egypt, he established that the heyday of the palace and the Minoan civilisation was round about 1700 BC; but in the year 1380 BC or thereabouts it was overwhelmed by some terrible catastrophe. What Evans did was to rebuild where necessary in order to give the public an impression of what this many-storeyed palace had been like before it was destroyed by fire or earthquake or both.

Schliemann had shown that there could often be a kernel of truth in the most unlikely-sounding legends. And in this palace that legend associated with the Minotaur, Evans was astonished to find evidence of bull-worship at every hand. There were bulls painted on frescoes, bulls' horns as symbols, bulls' hides stretched over warriors' shields. But, most astounding of all, one of the gaily-coloured frescoes suggested some acrobatic form of bull-sport, in which young men and girls somersaulted over the horns of a charging bull. Could this possibly have been the source of the

58

legend of the twelve Athenian youths and maidens sent to Crete each year to be sacrificed to the Minotaur?

As for the labyrinth—the palace *is* labyrinthine, a maze of apartments and offices surrounding a great central court. And then, in a tiny throne-room, Evans came across unmistakeable traces of a violent struggle. The chamber was a private royal shrine; could it be that in this sanctuary with its sunken lustral area the king of Knossos had once performed rituals wearing a bull-mask? In the room, the ceremonial basins were strewn about in disorder and there were scorch-marks on the wall—could the king have been interrupted in the middle of a last despairing appeal to the gods? It is all too tempting to imagine that the intruder must have been a warrior called Theseus, arriving at the head of a band of Greek raiders to overthrow the Cretan hegemony of the seas, and that he had now penetrated the palace labyrinth to face the bull-king in his den. Certainly, that is how the legend of Theseus and the Minotaur might well have been born. Sir Arthur Evans wrote:

Figurine of snake goddess found at Knossos

> 'We know now that the old traditions were true. We have before our eyes a wondrous spectacle—the resurgence, namely, of a civilisation twice as old as that of Hellas. It is true that on the old palace site what we see are only the ruins of ruins, but the whole is still inspired with Minos' spirit of order and organisation, and the free and natural art of the great architect Daedalus. The spectacle, indeed, that we have here before us is assuredly one of world-wide significance.'

Evans' instincts had been proved right. The Minoans emerged as the first truly civilised Europeans, with a history stretching back as far as 2500 BC, and the brilliance of their civilisation was superior to anything in the known world at the time. It preceded and to some extent influenced that of Mycenae, although in the end the Mycenaeans overran Crete for half a century.

But Evans suffered one major disappointment. In the ruins of the palace of Knossos he had found, as he had hoped, hundreds of clay tablets covered with Minoan inscriptions. But he found more than he bargained for—no fewer than three written scripts. There were very few examples of the early hieroglyphic script that had first engaged Evans' attention and which is still undeciphered. But there were two forms of syllabic scripts, which Evans named Linear A and Linear B. Linear A, the earlier script, has defied all efforts at decipherment. However, in 1952, when Sir Arthur Evans had been

01 ⊢ da   08 ⊣ a

02 ╪ ro   09 ᴽ se

03 ╪ pa   10 ⨍ u

04 ≢ te   11 ╕ po

05 ╤ to   12 ⫟ so

06 ⊼ na   13 ᴽ² me

07 ⫪ di   14 ꝑ do

Fourteen Linear B
signs, with their
numerical equivalents
and phonetic values

dead for ten years, Linear B was brilliantly deciphered by the late Michael Ventris and identified as an early form of Greek.

Sir Arthur Evans belongs to the Heroic Age of archaeology, though he worked in the twentieth century; he belongs to the school of the great private excavators. No one today could afford to pour such huge sums of money into archaeology as Schliemann or Evans did; no private individual could afford to restore a palace so expensively. Modern scholars tend to frown on Evans' work of restoration, preferring to leave a site without embellishment; but the palace of Knossos, as reconstructed, gives thousands of people every year a more vivid insight into the glittering, brilliant world of the Minoans than any excavation report could ever do.

SIR FLINDERS PETRIE

If any one man bridged the Heroic Age of archaeology and the more Scientific Age of today, it was Sir Flinders Petrie. A big black-bearded, formidable man, a man whom everyone is agreed to call a genius, if a somewhat errant one, he did more for Egyptology than any other archaeologist. He pushed back the frontiers of Egyptian history into a hitherto unknown past. He conducted excavations on a massive scale, his output of books and excavation reports was prodigious, he introduced a new and invaluable technique into archaeology known as *sequence dating*. And yet, by modern standards, his methods were primitive. That is a measure of how much archaeology has advanced in this century.

Born in 1853, he started his career as a metrologist—one who studies the science of measurements; his earliest work was an attempt to discover the unit of measurement used by the builders of Stonehenge. And it was this interest that first took him to Egypt as a young man in his twenties. His father, who was an electrical engineer and mathematician, had become enamoured of the quasi-magical theories of Piazzi Smyth, who interpreted the Great Pyramid at Giza as being a mystical computer whose precise dimensions concealed mathematically coded prophecies about the fate of the world. Petrie, at his father's request, spent two seasons surveying and studying the pyramids, in the course of which he demolished this occult theory with what he called one 'ugly little fact'—the actual measurements did not fit the required figures! But, much more significantly, the mission turned him into an Egyptologist.

Sir Flinders Petrie.

Standards had improved immeasurably since the days of Belzoni, but even so, Petrie was appalled by what he saw. The French archaeologist Auguste Mariette, who was appointed Conservator of Egyptian Monuments in 1858, had put a stop to the worst excesses of looting; but three years after Mariette's death in 1880, Petrie castigated him severely for the brutality and backwardness of his own methods—including the blasting of a ruined temple with dynamite:

> 'Nothing seems to be done with any uniform or regular plan. Work is begun and left unfinished, no regard is paid to future requirements of exploration and no civilised or labour-saving appliances are used, nothing but what the natives have ... It is sickening to see the rate at which everything is being destroyed, and the little regard paid to preservation. Anything would be better than leaving things to be destroyed wholesale; better spoil half in preserving the other half, than leave the whole to be smashed.'

Throughout his career, Petrie was more interested in developing the intellectual aspect of his subject than in finding rich treasures. He launched himself into excavation with furious energy, exploring pyramids, opening up tombs, discovering papyri. By 1900 he had established a proper chronology and king-lists for the first three Dynasties before the start of the Old Kingdom for which not a scrap of evidence had existed before 1880, and thereby he pushed the known history of Egypt back by nearly 500 years.

But before that he had conducted the least spectacular but perhaps most important of his innumerable excavations. In 1894, he opened a great prehistoric cemetery on the western bank of the Nile at a place called Naqada. It comprised some three thousand pit-graves, each containing a skeleton lying on its side in a crouched position and pottery of a type hitherto unknown. He did not identify the cemetery as being predynastic at first. He concentrated on the pottery, and it was this close study that led him to devise the technique of sequence dating. What gave him the clue was the fact that the wavy edges which served as hand-holds on some of the pottery degenerated into mere decorative marks on other pots, and this suggested to him that he should be able to plot the changes of form and style and type; by correlating several of these typologies he could build up a numbered sequence of burials, and any new burial could be equated with one of the numbers and thus given its relative position in the sequence. It was a revolutionary technique for its time, and enabled archaeologists to get some order and perspective into the blind years of Egyptian prehistory.

Pottery and cosmetic palette from Naqada

It was also a triumphant vindication of Petrie's passionate belief in the importance of the apparently valueless objects of archaeology compared with the obvious treasures. It was precisely because pottery was so cheap and worthless that it was such a valuable tool for the archaeologist. It was too cheap and easy to make to be worth transporting over long distances; it was too fragile to be likely to survive unbroken for long; it was too commonplace to be worth hoarding. Thus, any pottery in a tomb could be assumed to be a local and reasonably fresh product and, as such, a reliable touch-stone for dating purposes.

Petrie also conducted digs in Palestine; but it was with Egypt that his name will for ever be associated. His dig at El Amarna brought to light the strange and brilliant world of the 'heretic Pharaoh', Akhenaten, husband of the beautiful Queen Nefertiti. His excavation of the tombs of the First Dynasty kings at Abydos rescued the early history of this Osiris cult-centre from the destruction wrought by previous archaeologists. He seemed to be everywhere; and it was his sheer energy that led him into the lapses that modern archaeologists deplore. Petrie, the man who mercilessly criticised his predecessors for their slipshod work, himself worked with too much haste; he did not give himself time to supervise his excavations properly; he favoured mass-excavation that swept a whole area clean; he did not pay sufficient attention to the meticulous principles of stratigraphy laid down by Pitt Rivers; his publications though prompt were hurried and often cursory.

Throughout his 89 restless years Petrie was always in a hurry. In *Seventy Years in Archaeology* he recalled the sense of urgency that was forced upon him in his youth:

> 'The science of observation, of registration, of recording, was as yet unthought of; nothing had a meaning unless it were an inscription or a sculpture. A year's work in Egypt made me feel it was like a house on fire, so rapid was the destruction going on. My duty was that of a salvage man, to get all I could, quickly gathered, and then when I was sixty I would sit down and write it up. That was a true forecast.'

Bracelets found by Sir Flinders Petrie on the arm of a mummy from the tomb of King Djer at Abydos.

He continued to be a salvage man to the end of his life in 1942, digging and writing with unflagging zeal. Whatever his deficiencies, it is his greatness that is best remembered now.

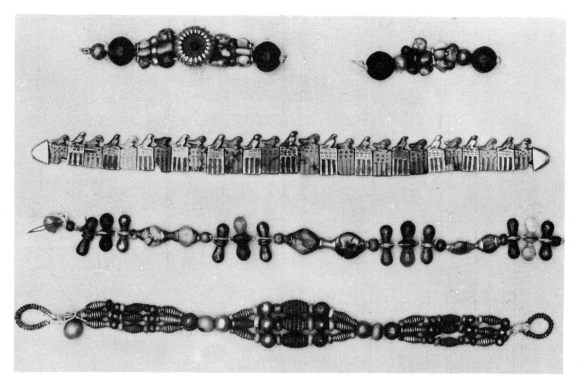

Silver rein ring from Ur, decorated with an onager in electrum

SIR LEONARD WOOLLEY

The first of the great twentieth-century excavators who liked to claim that he was the first archaeologist to make his living solely from archaeology was Sir Leonard Woolley (1880–1960), whose name will always be associated with the excavation of the royal Sumerian city of Ur of the Chaldees.

He had become an archaeologist purely by accident. The son of a clergyman, he had had no very clear idea of what he wanted to do after completing a First Class degree in theology at Oxford. It was the Warden of his college, Dr W. A. Spooner of Spoonerism fame, who made the decision for him by sending him to Sir Arthur Evans at the Ashmolean Museum to train to be an archaeologist.

He became a sub-curator at the Ashmolean, and for two years he was schooled by the great excavator of Knossos in museum techniques; cataloguing, cleaning, classifying the Minoan finds. Then in 1907, with no experience of field-work, he was suddenly thrust in charge of a Roman excavation at Corbridge in Northumberland. All his helpers were amateur:

> 'I know only too well that the work there would have scandalised, and rightly scandalised, any British archaeologist of today . . . In point of fact I had never so much as seen an excavation, I had never studied archaeological methods even from books . . . and I had not any idea of how to make a survey or a ground-plan, apart from being used to handling antiquities in a museum, and that only for a few months, I had no qualifications at all.'

But the excavation went well. Woolley unearthed a large quantity of Roman coins finer than anything of the sort found in Britain before that time, and he was commended for his care in the field. It was an auspicious start to the career of the first professional archaeologist.

Because of his theological training, Woolley always hoped that one day he might make a Biblical discovery of importance. He did some digging in Nubia, but in 1912 he was appointed to take over the British Museum expedition at Carchemish, in Mesopotamia. Carchemish was a site on the upper Euphrates not far from the modern city of Aleppo in northern Syria. It used to be the capital of the great Hittite empire which had successfully challenged the power of Assyria and Egypt in its time but had eventually fallen to Assyria in the eighth century BC.

After the First World War, during which he served as a British agent in the Middle East, Woolley continued his excavations in Mesopotamia. He made his name with some spectacular finds at the mound of Al' Ubaid, not far from Ur of the Chaldees, where he uncovered a splendid Sumerian temple complex of about 2600 BC, decorated with copper statues and reliefs and magnificent mosaic friezes of bulls, stags, and eagles. But it was the great mound of Tell Muqayyar, nearby, that was to give Woolley his greatest opportunity. It had been discovered and identified as the site of Ur of the Chaldees as early as 1854, but the joint British Museum/University Museum of Pennsylvania expedition that Woolley led throughout the 1920's was the first serious attempt to excavate it.

'We have found the Flood!' In 1929, that telegram to London from Woolley at Ur made headlines round the world. What prompted it was the discovery of a layer of river-clay, almost ten feet thick, that formed one of the strata of a shaft he sank into the mound of Ur. It proved that somewhere around 4000 BC the prehistoric settlement of Ur had been violently interrupted by a great inundation that had left this heavy deposit of water-borne clay. Woolley had jumped to the conclusion that this was evidence proving the Bible had been right—that there had once been a great deluge whose memory lingered in stories of Noah and the Flood.

Sir Leonard Woolley at Ur of the Chaldees.

'We have found the Flood!' Part of the light-coloured 'Flood deposit' level, just above a darker stratum containing evidence of earlier occupation.

But much more important were the finds that he had already made at a higher (i.e. later) level in the Royal Cemetery of the kings of Sumeria. He had excavated a series of stone tombs filled with beautiful objects—golden drinking cups and goblets, mother-of-pearl mosaics, lapis lazuli and silver—which had been heaped round the dead at the moment of burial. There was also unmistakeable evidence that when a king died, his whole court died with him; for in the vaults they found the skeletons of the royal attendants who had lain down to die with him, as well as waggons full of household furniture and the skeletons of oxen still in harness. These burials dated from the time when Ur was at the height of its power about 2500 BC.

Woolley also uncovered the homes of prosperous merchants from around 2000 BC; it led to long arguments about whether Abraham

Detail from the
'Standard of Ur'. The
king feasts with his
nobles to the sound of
music from a lyre
player and singer

had lived in a fine house before he left Ur, or, as the Bible relates, in a tent.

Woolley's fame as an archaeologist rests on the tremendous skill and care he showed in rescuing and restoring objects that might have otherwise crumbled away to nothing—marvellous objects like the double-sided blue and gold mosaic named 'The Standard of Ur'; or the harp from one of the royal tombs whose wood was completely decayed leaving only the decorations; or the Sumerian goat rearing on its hindlegs to snuff the foliage of a bush (which Woolley, with his Biblical enthusiasms, immediately christened the Ram Caught in a Thicket). His excavation reports were immensely detailed and scholarly—but he also had the gift of writing popular accounts of his discoveries, like *Ur of the Chaldees*, that brought archaeology to the general public more successfully than ever before.

5

The 20th Century (1)

THE DISCOVERY OF MACHU PICCHU

It is hard to believe that even in the twentieth century there should still have existed 'lost cities'—cities hidden away in ancient jungles or on remote mountain tops that modern man with his curiosity and his map-making skills had never found. But in 1911 one such lost city really did come to light, in Peru—the Inca city of Machu Picchu, high in the Andes Mountains.

Like the Maya and the Aztecs of Central America, the Incas were a highly civilised Indian nation who fell to the Spanish invaders in the sixteenth century. Properly speaking, the word Inca applies only to the race of kings who ruled the people of what is now Peru, but it has come to be applied to the native people as a whole. The Incas were sun-worshippers, and their kingdom was a highly organised bureaucracy based on socialistic principles—for everyone except the kings! They were a Bronze Age people, in that they had no iron tools or weapons; nor had they invented the wheel. Nonetheless, they built magnificent buildings of great stone blocks they manhandled into the mountains from valley quarries; and the closely organised agricultural system ensured a high standard of wealth for the rulers.

In 1530, the Inca kingdom was invaded by the Spanish adventurer Francisco Pizarro with a force of 180 men and 37 horses. And just as Cortés had conquered Mexico with a handful of men ten years previously, Pizarro managed to seize power after he had treacherously captured and executed the ruling Inca. Pizarro then occupied the Inca capital, Cuzco, and appointed a puppet Inca, Manco; Manco soon led a revolt, but the Bronze Age weapons of the Indians—the spears and slings and bows and arrows—were no

68

match for the steel swords and firearms of the Spaniards. So Manco and the remains of his army marched into the valley of the Urubamba River and from there climbed to the inaccessible mountain-tops where the Incas were said to have an impregnable fortress. There, Manco and his successors held out for forty years, until the last of the Incas was captured by the Spaniards in the jungle and put to death in Cuzco; but no white man ever penetrated the mountains far enough to see the fortress of Vilcabamba, as the old chronicles called it. And when even the nineteenth-century explorers and map-makers failed to find it, people began to assume that it must have been a mere legend.

But a young teacher from Yale University, Hiram Bingham, thought differently. He was not an archaeologist by training; he was a historian and anthropologist who had become fascinated by the Incas, and a keen mountaineer and explorer. In 1911, he organised a Yale University expedition to Peru to collect geological, geographical and biological information—and try to find the 'lost capital of the Incas'.

He had the old Spanish chronicles to guide him, and the accounts

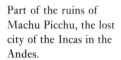

Part of the ruins of Machu Picchu, the lost city of the Incas in the Andes.

of the nineteenth-century explorers. With his team of experts he plunged on muleback into the jungle of the valley of the Urubamba River. It was wild country, which had only just been made accessible by the cutting of a road through the gorge of the river—before that, the native Indians had had to crawl along ledges and swing along by means of hanging vines. Because of this, earlier mapmakers had missed out a vast region, some 1,500 square miles in extent, whose existence was totally unsuspected, containing a great chain of snow-covered mountains. It was in these mountains that Bingham found his lost city.

The peak of Machu Picchu was unmarked on any map. But a local Indian told Bingham that there were some interesting ruins on top. On the morning of July 24, 1911, Bingham set off with two Indian guides—the other members of the expedition felt disinclined to go on such an exhausting climb. It was a very difficult climb indeed, in steamy heat, scrambling up almost vertical slopes. Suddenly, on a saddle between two peaks, he stumbled out of a bamboo thicket and found himself amongst buildings—fine, curved buildings with walls of pure white granite, carefully keyed into the natural rock. The Indians kept urging Bingham to climb higher and higher. He came to a great granite stairway that led to two massive temples made of huge blocks of dressed stone each weighing ten tons or more. There was an extensive courtyard, flanked by another temple with three great windows; elaborate terraces everywhere; and at the 'city-limits', the edge of the saddle-ridge—a sheer drop of some 1,500 feet to the thundering river at the bottom of the gorge. It was a site of staggering magnificence, a city that had once held about 2,000 people, impregnable to outside attack, for half a dozen men could easily have held the only approach path across the mountains. This was where the last of the Incas had held out after the Conquest, until the people had abandoned the city in despair.

Bingham returned the following year for a full-scale excavation and study of the houses that remained intact after four centuries. They found cemeteries containing mummified bodies, a reminder that a dead Inca ruler's mummy was looked after for years by members of his household as if he were still alive.

Today there is a single-track railroad up the valley of the Urubamba, and a bus that labours up to the ridge in bottom gear. A tourist hotel perches on the top beside the city ruins. The modern traveller can visit in comparative comfort now the city whose existence only sixty years ago was barely suspected.

THE TOMB OF TUTANKHAMUN

The Valley of the Kings in Egypt is a gash of sunburnt limestone in the Theban mountains. There is sand everywhere; the cooling Nile lies hidden behind a screen of raw cliffs. Here, more than 3,000 years ago, the most powerful rulers on earth chose to be buried in elaborate tunnelled tombs: 49 Egyptian kings were laid to rest here in their sumptuously decorated sepulchres. It was here, in 1922, that archaeology witnessed the most spectacular find ever made: the Tomb of Tutankhamun.

It was all the more dramatic for being unexpected. Most Egyptologists were convinced by then that all the royal tombs in the Valley of the Kings had been found and excavated. Besides, all the tombs had been rifled by tomb-robbers many centuries earlier, so the priceless treasures that had been buried with the dead pharaohs had all vanished long ago. But there was a faint chance that there was at least one more tomb hidden beneath the scree of the mountain-slopes, the tomb of the boy-king Tutankhamun, successor to the 'heretic Pharaoh', Akhenaten; and Lord Carnarvon, a wealthy English sportsman and enthusiast, was determined to find it.

There was little evidence to go on. It was known that after the reign of the sun-worshipping Akhenaten, who had brought about a religious revolution, his son-in-law Tutankhamun had ruled for nine years as a political puppet while the old religious order was being restored. It was also known that after Tutankhamun's death he was deliberately discredited, and earlier excavators had found funerary debris with his name inscribed on it thrown down a small pit in the Valley. It was assumed, therefore, that his tomb had been robbed soon after the burial; but a few optimists, including Lord Carnarvon, still believed that a secret burial place might have survived intact.

Gold and glass-paste pectoral found with Tutankhamun's mummy. The serpent-goddess of the North of Egypt and the vulture-goddess of the South flank the sacred eye

Lord Carnarvon had professional help in his search—a former draughtsman called Howard Carter who had been trained by Sir Flinders Petrie and others in making drawings of archaeological finds and had graduated into an archaeologist in his own right. Together, Lord Carnarvon and Carter searched the Valley of the Kings for five laborious seasons. In the summer of 1922, Lord Carnarvon decided that despite his great wealth he could not afford to finance yet another season. Howard Carter, however, begged for just one more; there was still one triangular area left unexplored, just below the entrance to the tomb of Ramesses VI where workmen's huts had been erected in antiquity. Carter asked for time to dig this last area, and Lord Carnarvon agreed. So Carter went to Egypt that autumn for what was intended to be his last season in the Valley of the Kings. Nine days later, Lord Carnarvon got one of those dramatic telegrams that punctuate the history of archaeology:

'At last have made wonderful discovery in Valley; a magnificent tomb with seals intact; re-covered same for your arrival; congratulations.'

On the morning of November 4, just a few days after the start of the dig, Carter had arrived at the site to be greeted with an expectant silence. Just two yards from where a previous excavator had stopped work, a step hewn in the rock had been uncovered. It was only thirteen feet below the entrance to the tomb of Ramesses VI. The step was the first of sixteen that plunged steeply through the rock. At the bottom was a doorway which had been blocked up with stones and plastered over. There were royal seals on it, later to be identified as those of Tutankhamun. With remarkable self-restraint, Carter filled in the stairway again and sent the cable to his sponsor. It was November 6, 1922.

Lord Carnarvon arrived three weeks later. But no one was sure what to expect on the far side of the door, for although parts of the wall were intact, there were others which had been broken and re-sealed, suggesting that intruders in ancient times had tunnelled down the staircase and broken in. There was therefore a distinct possibility that this tomb, like all the others in the Valley, had been stripped already.

On November 25, the door was pulled down. Behind it lay another rubble-choked corridor some 30 feet long. They cleared this sloping passage to a second door that had also been opened, re-blocked, and resealed. It was the door to the antechamber of the tomb. Howard Carter described the final moments of suspense on November 26:

'At last we had the whole door clear before us. The decisive moment had arrived. With trembling hands I made a tiny breach in the upper left-hand corner. Darkness and blank space, as far as an iron testing-rod could reach ... Candle tests were applied as a precaution against possible foul gases, and then, widening the hole a little, I inserted the candle and peered in, Lord Carnarvon

OPPOSITE
Howard Carter, crouching, examines the gilded shrines that lay inside one another like Chinese boxes.

... standing anxiously beside me to hear the verdict. At first I could see nothing, the hot air escaping from the chamber causing the candleflame to flicker, but presently, as my eyes grew accustomed to the light, details of the room within emerged slowly from the mist, strange animals, statues, and gold—everywhere the glint of gold. For the moment—an eternity it must have seemed to the others standing by—I was struck dumb with amazement; and when Lord Carnarvon, unable to stand the suspense any longer, inquired anxiously, "Can you see anything?" it was all I could do to get out the words, "Yes, wonderful things." '

Compared with some of the tombs in the Valley of the Kings—those of Ramesses VI, for instance, or Sethos I, ablaze with vividly-coloured frescoes and carvings from floor to ceiling, gallery upon gallery stretching deep into the mountain—Tutankhamun's tomb is unprepossessing in the extreme: small, relatively undecorated, obviously built in haste, as befitted a boy-king who had not had time to grow into authority and wealth. What has made this insignificant ruler into perhaps the most celebrated pharaoh in ancient Egyptian history was the accident that his tomb, alone of them all, had not been robbed. It had been broken into—but the thieves had been disturbed before they had had time to plunder it, and the priests had sealed it up again. For more than 3,000 years the young king's funeral treasures had lain untouched until that momentous day in the winter of 1922.

In the antechamber into which Howard Carter had peered lay a great jumble of precious things: gilded couches, a gold and silver throne, pieces of gold-plated chariots, boxes of preserved food for funerary feasts, hundreds of precious objects and vessels lying about in the disarray which the robbers had caused. For two painstaking months, Carter patiently cleared the ante-chamber of its crammed treasures, photographing, drawing, cataloguing and treating every object one by one on the spot before sending it off to Cairo—knowing all the time that the actual burial chamber next door contained probably even more spectacular treasures. And all the time the world's Press lay in wait outside the tunnel, racing to and fro on camels and donkeys in their haste to file news of the latest dramatic finds.

Then, on February 17, 1923, Carter and Lord Carnarvon broke into the burial chamber proper. It was almost entirely filled by a great gilded shrine. Two other rooms, the Treasury and the Annexe,

Detail from the gilded shrine:
Tutankhamun's queen

Howard Carter
cleaning the third
coffin of Tutankhamun
as it lies inside the
opened second coffin.

were also crammed with unbelievable riches—gilded chests and caskets and furniture, statues, urns, jewellery.

The huge shrine in the burial chamber contained three other shrines inside it, like Chinese boxes. Inside the fourth of the shrines, which was also made of gilded wood and highly decorated, there was a huge sarcophagus of yellow quartzite; and inside this stone coffin there were three more coffins, one inside the other, all fashioned in the shape of a mummy. The first was of gilded wood; the second, which fitted into it precisely, was also made of wood covered with gold leaf. The innermost coffin was made of solid gold, and weighed almost 300 lb; the lid represented the king in full regalia, and inside, the mummified body was studded with golden jewels and wore a beautiful golden face mask—the face of Tutankhamun.

Excavating and clearing the tomb took six years in all, years in which quarrels and lawsuits with the Egyptian authorities seriously interrupted operations. It all ended harmoniously, however; today the stone coffin is in its place in the burial chamber with the king's mummified body inside, whereas all the treasure, including the coffin of solid gold, is on display to the public in the Cairo Museum —not just the richest but the most superbly artistic treasure ever found in Egypt.

It is ironic that Lord Carnarvon himself did not live to see the sarcophagus opened. He died of pneumonia in April 1923, after a mosquito bite had turned septic. His death, coming so soon after the opening of the tomb, gave birth to a new Egyptian legend in the newspapers—the legend of a Pharaoh's Curse that strikes down those who violate a tomb.

The top of one of Tutankhamun's rings: the Pharaoh faces the falcon-headed god Horus as he sits on a throne, flanked by the sacred falcon and vulture

SCYTHIAN EXCAVATIONS

Throughout the 1920s the archaeological excitements in Egypt and Mesopotamia tended to overshadow news from other parts of the world. But in 1929, archaeologists in Russia opened a new chapter of their prehistory when they started excavating a frozen cemetery of Scythian princes.

The Scythians were a fierce nomadic people who roamed the steppes of Russia north of the Black Sea on horseback some 2,500 years ago, when classical Greek civilisation was at its peak. The Scythians were the first of the Iron Age Russians and had close trade contacts with Greece. Throughout the nineteenth century many handsome gold and silver objects of Scythian origin had been found in scattered burial mounds, but these had attracted little attention in the Western world compared with Schliemann's finds at Troy and Mycenae.

Little was known about the Scythians apart from an account written by the Greek historian of the fifth century BC, Herodotus, after he had visited the steppes. In particular, he had described their burial customs:

Carved wooden stag with leather antlers from Pazyryk

> 'Then the body of the dead king is laid in a grave, stretched upon a mattress. Spears are fixed in the ground on either side of the corpse, and beams stretched across above it to form a roof, which is covered with thatching. In the open space around the body of the king they bury one of his concubines, and also his cup-bearer, his cook, his groom, his lackey, his messenger, some of his horses . . . and some golden cups. After this they set to work and raise a vast mound above the grave.'

In 1929, the Soviet archaeologist C. I. Rudenko led an expedition from the State Ethnographical Museum high into the Altai Mountains in Siberia, where a group of burial mounds had been discovered in a valley called Pazyryk. They were at an altitude of 1,650 metres above sea-level; but although Pazyryk is not ice-bound all the year round, by some freak of climate the ground underneath the barrows had become permanently frozen. As a result, the burial chambers had been preserved in perpetuity just as they had been left by the tomb-robbers who removed the valuables soon after the burials. The loss of the treasures was much less important than the fact that the ice had preserved things that normally leave no trace in tombs—

Stylised animal forms like this ornament of a panther were a feature of Scythian goldwork.

flesh, textiles, furs, and wood. So the archaeologists were enabled to see how a tomb was furnished at the time of the funeral—and from this there emerged startling confirmation of the account by Herodotus.

Six barrows were excavated in that 1929 season and again in 1947 and 1949. In each case, a tomb shaft led down into a large log-framed burial chamber some 24 metres square—walls, floor and ceiling all lined with double thicknesses of timber. The roof was

78

thatched with many layers of birch-bark. The coffins were enormous, hollowed out of tree-trunks five metres long. Three embalmed bodies had survived the attentions of the tomb-robbers, two men and a woman.

The tombs were thought of as being literally 'houses of the dead'; and the way they were furnished was meant to correspond to real houses. So as the archaeologists carefully chipped out the ice, they were in effect thawing out chambers such as Scythian nobles of the fifth century BC would have lived as well as died in.

These cut-out leather cock silhouettes from Pazyryk were used to decorate the rim of a coffin

On the floor were carpets—the oldest surviving deep-pile carpets in the world, covered with rich designs, with figures of animals in the broad ornamental borders. There were also felt carpets and wall-hangings, and these, too, were decorated with lively scenes of animal art. There were clothes of silk from China and woollen cloth from central Asia; but most striking of all were the horsecloths, vividly decorated with scenes of animals fighting, and a large collection of elegantly carved wooden plates used as harness ornaments.

Next to the burial chamber were the horse burials, just as Herodotus had described. There was a four-wheeled waggon that had been used for the cortège, and beside it the bodies of many horses splendidly caparisoned. They had been in excellent condition, and analysis of the stomach contents showed they had been fed on grain. These were the chieftain's thoroughbred riding horses.

The chief himself lay in his coffin; and nearby, as Herodotus had suggested, lay the embalmed body of a woman. The men had been elaborately tattooed with animal forms. One of the chiefs had been killed in battle, his skull shattered and scalped, but his men had recovered the tattooed body and given it a proper funeral here with his possessions and domestic comforts all around him. Herodotus had described a festive practice at funerals, whereby the Scythians got drunk by inhaling the vapour of roasted hemp seeds in a portable booth made of poles and felt; Rudenko found a cauldron with heating stones and hemp seeds, and a bundle of poles and felt sheeting.

Leather stag cut-out silhouette from Pazyryk

After the funeral, the tomb shafts had been filled up with logs, each one six metres long—sometimes as many as three hundred of them. At some later date, thieves had broken through this log-jam and stolen the most valuable of the ornaments; but by their entry they allowed water to seep down the shafts into the chambers, where it turned into permanent ice to preserve the burials for posterity.

THE SUTTON HOO SHIP

The most important pre-war find in northern Europe was made in England in 1939, in a group of mounds near the River Deben at Woodbridge, in Suffolk, six miles from the sea. Inside one mound were the shadowy remains of a great Anglo-Saxon warship and a hoard of treasure reminiscent of the Anglo-Saxon epic poem *Beowulf*:

> 'Deep in the ship they laid him down,
> Their beloved lord, the giver of rings,
> The hero by the mast. Great treasures there,
> Far-gathered trappings were taken and set:
> No ship in fame more fittingly furnished
> With weapons of war and battle-armour,
> With mail-coat and sword; there lay to his hand
> Precious things innumerable to go at his side,
> Voyaging to the distant holds of the flood.'

The excavation of what has become known as the Sutton Hoo Ship began, as so many of the most celebrated excavations have done, rather diffidently. There were eleven mounds on the site. In 1938 the landowner, Mrs E. M. Pretty, hired a part-time employee of the Ipswich Museum, Basil Brown, to investigate the mounds, paying him £1.50 a week. He dug into three of the smaller mounds and found little, but sufficient to prove they were of Anglo-Saxon origin; and one of them seemed to contain traces of a ship.

The following year, with the help of Mrs Pretty's gardener, he tackled the largest of the mounds. And soon, in the middle of May, he and the gardener came across some iron bolts. They were the rivets of the bow of a huge ship some eighty feet long. None of the wood had survived. It had all rotted away, leaving the iron bolts in their original position in the sandy soil—and a strange impression on the sand, like a photographic negative, of all the vanished timbers.

At this point the authorities moved in and a team of professional archaeologists led by C. W. Phillips took over, for this was clearly the largest Anglo-Saxon ship ever found in Britain, and because it was so far from the sea it was obviously part of a ship-burial of the kind described in *Beowulf*. Unlike the great ship-burials in Norway, the Sutton Hoo Ship had not been plundered, giving us a

OPPOSITE
'The Ram Caught in a Thicket' from the Royal Cemetery, Ur: figure of a male goat with its forefeet in the branches of a tree.

The goddess Isis in protective role shields the smaller gilded shrine which contained the internal organs of Tutankhamun.

glimpse of the kind of wealth that had been stolen from the royal funerals of Viking times.

They started digging amidships, where any burial chamber might be expected to be found. And on Sunday, July 22, one of the excavators uncovered a superb gold-and-garnet ornament, the first of a hoard of jewellery of great artistry and beauty. They had found a royal burial, the ship-funeral of some seventh-century Anglo-Saxon king. Day after day throughout that uneasy summer of 1939 more and more treasures came to light, all the magnificent regalia of royalty. There was a ceremonial iron standard and a whetstone, and a number of seven-foot spears. Of armour there was a sword embellished with gold and studded with garnets, a gold-embossed shield, an iron helmet inlaid with silver wires; a great golden belt-buckle for the baldric—solid gold, weighing fourteen ounces, and still in perfect working order; jewelled wrist-clasps and a heap of lesser buckles and scabbard bosses. There was a magnificent decorated purse of solid gold filled with 37 Merovingian gold coins; a belt studded with more than 4,000 cut garnets; a great silver dish from Byzantium, a nest of nine silver bowls; silver spoons and drinking horns; and innumerable other objects of bronze and wood, including the crushed remains of a musical instrument thought to be a harp but now brilliantly reconstituted as a lyre.

There was only time to get the treasures out and stored away in safety before war broke out in September 1939. There was no time to do more than fill the trench with bracken. During the war the area was used as a training-ground for tanks, and the Sutton Hoo mound was picked out as one of the obstacles to be negotiated!

The bracken in the trench rotted down and five feet of soil silted over it. 25 years later, experts from the British Museum re-excavated the mound—not to look for more treasure, but to study once again, with the advantage of new scientific techniques, the ghost-like impression of the vanished timbers, in order to try to establish the exact dimensions of the ship.

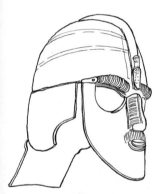

The reconstructed iron helmet, Sutton Hoo

Miraculously, very little damage had occurred; the gunwales at the prow had been crushed by the weight of tanks passing over it, and the starboard side had split towards the stern, but that was all. And so began the second stage of the Sutton Hoo excavation—less dramatic, certainly, but showing how increased skills and more refined techniques can extract more information from a site than a previous generation of archaeologists would have thought possible.

Silver spoon, Sutton Hoo

The trench was bared and photographed from above using a

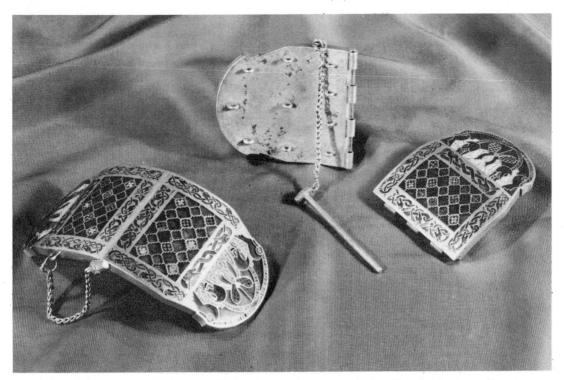

The pair of hinged gold shoulder-clasps with garnet and enamel decoration from the Sutton Hoo Ship.

General view of the excavation of the Anglo-Saxon warship at Sutton Hoo. Only the iron bolts were left in the soil, the timbers had rotted away.

technique called *photogrammetry;* it is the method used to make maps by joining together a series of matching aerial photographs. The position of all the iron bolts was carefully plotted. Some new things were found—one of the oars, for instance, and traces of gold leaf. And then the great boat was excavated to destruction, safe in the knowledge that a complete record was now available, in the form of a full-scale plaster cast of the imprint of the vessel in the soil. Six tons of plaster-of-Paris were used; and from this cast, British Museum technicians have made a fibre-glass mould of the boat as it was found. If a wooden replica of the ship is ever built, like the replica of the Norwegian Gokstad ship that was sailed across the Atlantic in 1893, it would be simple to construct now; but it would not be quite so simple to run—the Sutton Hoo ship was propelled by 38 oars, and there was no mast or sail to do the work!

No body was ever found in the ship, and it is now believed that the Sutton Hoo ship was in fact a cenotaph rather than a burial. Historians think it likely that the burial was associated with a seventh-century king of East Anglia called Aethelhere who was killed at the Battle of Winwaed in Northumbria on November 15, 665 AD. His body was never found; it was probably swept away by flood waters near where the battle was fought. It seems not unlikely that the empty grave-ship at Sutton Hoo was laid in his honour, a burial without a body but with full royal rites. The identification may not be correct; but the brilliance and beauty of the royal treasure now on show in the King Edward VII Gallery of the British Museum brings the old poetry vividly to life, and suggests a remarkably wealthy and cultured society for those early times.

6

The 20th Century (2)

Archaeology has made tremendous progress since the Second World War. New techniques, new scientific aids and new interpretative skills have all combined to revolutionise this relatively young subject, and to add enormously to our knowledge of the past.

THE CIVILISATION OF THE INDUS VALLEY

One of the new techniques was a method of excavation pioneered by Sir Mortimer Wheeler, particularly during his work in the Indus Valley in the 1940s when he was Director-General of Archaeology in India. There he helped to reveal an unsuspected prehistoric civilisation in India—and, incidentally, to find echoes of fact in the 'mythical' collection of Hindu Sanskrit writings known as the *Rigveda*. The technique is the so-called 'square' method of tackling excavations, instead of the old-fashioned trenches or *sondages* with which men like Schliemann used to attack a site. It involves digging in a series of squares, like a grid, about twenty or thirty feet square, with a balk or strip of undug earth left between adjacent squares. This gives the archaeologist much greater control of the dig; each individual square remains a clearly defined sub-unit of the whole dig, a dig in miniature, as it were, with all the stratification of the site outlined in detail, and this makes his task much easier when it comes to the vital job of recording the excavation for eventual publication. The balks themselves, of two or three feet in width, afford access to and from the squares for diggers and wheelbarrows; and the archaeologist can extend the system of squares in any direction he wants as new information comes to light, without disturbing an area that has already been dug.

When he was working in India, Wheeler applied this precise and orderly method with striking success when he re-excavated two great mounds that concealed the twin capitals of the long-lost people of the Indus civilisation: the cities of Harappa, in the Punjab, and Mohenjo-Daro, some four hundred miles to the south-west on the banks of the Indus. Fifty years ago, the existence of this ancient civilisation had only been guessed at from myths and legends; but excavations in the 1920s and 1930s revealed that an advanced civilisation contemporary with those of ancient Sumeria and Egypt had flourished over an enormous area stretching from the Arabian Gulf to Delhi, centred on the valley of the Indus and covering about half a million square miles.

In the *Rigveda* the Aryan invaders who had swept into India around 1500 BC had as their paramount god a leader called Indra, who was called 'the fort-destroyer', who 'destroyed ninety forts and a hundred ancient castles'. These 'forts' were thought to be legendary; until the precision of Wheeler's new technique enabled him to see what earlier archaeologists had missed—traces of immensely thick mudbrick fortifications.

The cities laid bare by the square technique dated from about 2000 or 2500 BC. They were extremely well organised, laid out in careful squares like a grid—an urban planner's dream, in fact. Each city had enough housing to accommodate about 35,000 people, and each had a fortified citadel with walls of mudbrick forty feet thick and an external skin of burnt-brick. This citadel was on a platform, and within it were all the public buildings—an enormous sunken bath or tank with an elaborate drainage system for ritual ablutions, and a suite of rooms around it; a huge granary; a block of offices. The town proper spread out round the citadel in a series of standardised street blocks, each of which contained a huddle of peasant houses and shops and craft workshops. Oddly enough, no trace of anything resembling a temple was found. But there was a number of circular working platforms on which an organised labour force had pounded grain. It is quite clear that within these cities there was a rigid class division between the coolies and the middle-class traders who monopolised the wealth, which is not unlike the conservative, sedentary pattern of caste-systems in the social life of India today.

In these ancient cities, life was well-ordered, disciplined, efficient, and above all sanitary, as Wheeler noted in *The Indus Age:*

'The noteworthy and recurrent features are the insistence on water-supply, bathing and drainage. In some houses a built seat-latrine of Western type is included on the ground or first floor, with a sloping and sometimes stepped channel through the wall to a pottery receptacle or brick drain in the street outside.'

A typical street in Mohenjo-Daro after excavation, showing the standardised blocks of housing.

All this information has had to be inferred from the archaeological evidence alone, for no one has yet been able to decipher the writings found on the Indus Valley trading seals by which wealth was exchanged with Mesopotamia and the Arabian Gulf through the ancient commercial centre of Dilmun (modern Bahrein).

One of the many unsolved mysteries of the Indus civilisation is why a people so technically advanced in social and urban organisation produced so little art of any quality. Apart from a very few small masterpieces on display in the National Museum at New Delhi, Indus workmanship was wholly undistinguished and utilitarian—as dull and standardised as their townscapes.

But their ultimate fate seems clear enough now, as revealed by the sacred writings and the archaeologist's sensitive spade; for at one level the streets and houses were littered with dead, their skulls smashed by sword-blows, women and children butchered in their homes by the Aryan invaders led by their god-chief Indra: 'He rends forts as age consumes a garment,' says the *Rigveda*. 'Indra stands accused,' says Wheeler. 'Literary (or rather oral) tradition and archaeological inference have apparently more in common with each other than had previously been suspected.'

THE SEARCH FOR CAMELOT

Despite the new professionalism, the tendency to want to identify, to create stories, to relate objects to names, is still very strong: archaeology is digging up people, not things. The professionals are apt to think it unscientific, remembering Schliemann and all the blunders that have been made by over-hasty identifications; but nonetheless it remains a very real feeling. For instance, there is the extraordinary response that the name 'Camelot' seems to arouse.

No archaeologist believes in the Camelot of King Arthur as a physical place where Arthur and his Knights of the Round Table had their headquarters. In that sense, Camelot is a romantic medieval fiction. But a lot of people believe in King Arthur, and there are societies devoted to his memory, even though the historical evidence for his existence is rather slight. It is merely a possibility, no more, that there was a Romano-British war leader of the early sixth century called Arthur (Artorius) who united the British tribes against the invading Saxons and temporarily halted their progress. After his death he became a symbol of a lost golden age, a legendary champion of his people and of Christianity. In the centuries that followed, the fame of Arthur flourished in the fastnesses to which the Britons had retreated—in Wales, in Cornwall, in Cumberland, even across the Channel in Brittany.

By the twelfth century, King Arthur had been adopted officially into history; the court historian Geoffrey of Monmouth, intent on inventing a respectable genealogy for the Norman rulers of England, recruited this obscure British folk-hero and elevated him into an emperor of Christendom, defender of the faith, keeper of the Holy Grail, paragon of courtly chivalry, and by patriotic extension the symbol of everything good about being British.

So potent is the spell of Arthur to this day that the merest whisper of his name in association with an archaeological project is sufficient to raise the necessary funds. The most unlikely excavations have been financed by Arthurian enthusiasts, from Tintagel in Cornwall to the lowlands of Scotland; and when Sir Mortimer Wheeler was excavating the Roman amphitheatre at Caerleon in Monmouthshire, the chance mention of the fact that this overgrown oval hollow in the ground was known locally as 'King Arthur's Round Table' inspired members of the American Round Table to underwrite the costs of excavating and restoring Roman Caerleon as a national monument.

The latest claimant to the title of Camelot has been the imposing, 500-foot-high hill-fort of South Cadbury in Somerset. The excavator, Leslie Alcock of University College, Cardiff, prefers to blame newspaper romanticists for emphasising the Arthurian associations of a site whose history stretches four thousand years from Neolithic to late Saxon occupation, but the appeal for funds published by the Camelot Research Committee made no bones about it: 'Only work on this scale will enable us to recover the plan and appearance of Camelot, the real city that lies behind the Arthurian Romances of the Middle Ages.'

The excavation of South Cadbury went on for five summers, from 1966 to 1970, and proved to be a great success, both academically and from the popular point of view. The excavation involved a huge geophysical survey of the eighteen acres of this windswept hilltop, in which no fewer than 100,000 readings were made by instruments that located man-made disturbances under the surface of the ground by measuring the magnetic field of the earth. This allowed the excavators to direct their attention to the most promising areas of the site.

Over the seasons, the long story of South Cadbury gradually emerged. The earliest occupants were settlers in the late Neolithic period, c. 3000 BC, who left traces of pits and hearths with pottery and flints. There was extensive resettlement of the site in the pre-Roman Iron Age, when Celtic tribesmen lived on the hilltop and built a township there. They also built formidable defences against rival tribesmen—four great ramparts of earth, stone, and timber. There was evidence that the fortifications were refurbished on the eve of the Roman Conquest, c. 45 AD, but to no avail. The Romans stormed the gateway; the key and hinges and strappings of the door lay on the ground near the kerb-stones that had been grooved by the wheels of countless chariots; and all around was evidence of the slaughter the Romans inflicted on the inhabitants.

After the Roman destruction of the fort, life slowly returned to South Cadbury. By the late Saxon period, in the tenth and eleventh centuries, it was an important burgh. But it was the Arthurian evidence that naturally attracted most attention, for it became clear that in the period associated with Arthur, *c.* 500 AD, the defences had been carefully repaired, and the hill-top was occupied by a powerful and wealthy British family. The climax of the excavation came with the discovery in 1969 of an extensive pattern of post-holes in the ground that marked out the remains of a large Arthurian hall or wooden palace: the palace of Arthur's Camelot!

It is all too easy to leap to conclusions and see in one's mind's eye the figure of Arthur thundering out through the gate of South Cadbury at the head of a force of heavy cavalry to engage the marauding Saxons in a series of skirmishes that earned him his immortality; but Leslie Alcock is more circumspect, and contents himself with saying:

'It is very tempting to think that it (South Cadbury) must have played a special role in the military affairs of southern England in the generations around 500 AD.'

INDUSTRIAL ARCHAEOLOGY

One of the newest branches of archaeology, which has developed entirely since the Second World War, is industrial archaeology: the study of industrial monuments of the last two hundred years or so. The word itself was only coined in the mid-fifties; but it has grown very fast in popular appeal and participation.

Much of the appeal of industrial archaeology lies in the fact that anyone can participate without any specialist training—all one needs is a passion for old machinery and a capacity for hard work. What is at stake is the industrial heritage of countries, threatened with destruction by the pace of modernisation in industry and transport and urban redevelopment. The industrial archaeologist wants to preserve where possible examples of early industrial machinery and building, but if preservation is impossible then at least to build up a complete record of it.

There is no end to the subjects that come under the heading of industrial archaeology: the development of the coal trade, of textile manufacture, of railways and canals, of sources of power, of the dark

The Naval Boat Stores at Sheerness, completed in 1860, is the earliest multi-storey iron framed building in existence, the ancestor of the modern skyscraper.

satanic mills that created the economic strengths of the nineteenth century.

Tower Bridge in London is a working example of nineteenth-century engineering at its height. It was opened in 1894, and the bridge is opened and closed by steam power. Enormous steam engines are used to pump water to the hydraulic engines that raise and lower the mighty bascules. Sometime in the future this fine bridge will become obsolete, as the movement of the docks further down river means that the staff of seventy who superintend the bridge are required to open it less and less frequently; the industrial archaeologist believes it is his duty to ensure that it is preserved. The same goes for the world's first cast-iron bridge that spans the River Severn, built in 1779, with main ribs weighing over eighty tons. It was the world's first prefabricated metal structure, and has been called the Stonehenge of the Industrial Revolution.

Some enthusiasts just want to see fine old engines in good working order. Others find satisfaction in building up museums of the industrial past—open-air museums of living history like Skansen at Stockholm, which concentrates on the rural crafts of the past, or

Beamish Hall in County Durham which reflects the industrial history of the North of England.

Members of local societies devote hours of leisure time to recording, repairing, studying, photographing and cleaning all these aspects of our more recent past. But it is not merely a sentimental pursuit. First-hand knowledge of this kind gives a practical dimension to history that no textbook can offer. To stroll through the model village of New Lanark, founded in Scotland by Robert Owen in 1799 as a workers' Utopia, is to meet the Industrial Revolution face to face as a fact and not merely a historical concept.

Some professional archaeologists still tend to think of industrial archaeology as a poor relation, a non-academic and undisciplined activity. But it plays its part in preserving a vital part of the cultural heritage of any community, however recent, and it can be a powerful teaching aid in schools—as well as being a source of great enjoyment, for it is above all an activity for the lay enthusiast. There is now a great and growing number of local industrial archaeological societies which are always happy to welcome willing new recruits.

UNDERWATER ARCHAEOLOGY

Another branch that is growing rapidly in popularity is underwater archaeology, thanks to the development of the aqualung. Regrettably, because there is not sufficient legislation to protect wreck-sites, there is still a great deal of treasure-hunting and looting involved on the part of swimmers only interested in finding pieces-of-eight. Irreparable damage has been done to historic wrecks by treasure-seekers who are prepared to dynamite their way to a fortune if necessary.

But underwater archaeology has had its distinguished recruits, like the celebrated Belgian diver Robert Stenuit who located the wreck of a Spanish Armada ship, the *Girona*, off the north-west coast of Ireland in 1969. Stenuit spent many months studying the historical records in the archives of Europe, on the basis of which he was able to make a positive identification of the wreck when he found the remains in a cove on the Irish coast. The *Girona* was a galleass, fleeing homewards in 1588 with 1300 men on board—the survivors of three ships' crews. On the night of October 26, in a furious storm, she was driven onto the rocks of Lacade Point and ripped open. Only five men of that 1300 managed to get to shore alive; many of the others had been so weighted down with gold and jewellery that they had not a chance.

Stenuit took a team of professional divers to Ireland and searched the seabed with meticulous care. They found a fortune in golden ornaments and coins; but, more significantly, Stenuit was able to identify the ship positively because of the care with which the position of all the finds was plotted, and by his knowledge of the period; he was able to relate pieces of personal jewellery to members of the ship's crew known to have been on board at the time. Ironically, the definite identification of the wreck has served to enhance the cash value of the finds, for a Spanish doubloon known to have come from a particular Armada ship such as the *Girona* would attract a higher price than an anonymous coin of the same period.

Recovering objects, particularly perishable objects, after long immersion in salt or clear water is a very difficult and delicate task, quite apart from the physical dangers and limitations involved for the divers. But the technical problems of recovery are gradually being overcome, and some classic recoveries have now been made. The seventeenth-century Swedish man-of-war *Vasa* was successfully salvaged and is on display in Stockholm. In 1960, a Mycenean merchant ship of the thirteenth century BC was discovered on the seabed off Cape Gelidonya in southwest Turkey, and its cargo of copper ingots from Cyprus successfully recovered.

In Denmark, the recent recovery of a small fleet of ships of the Viking Age demonstrates the great advances that are being made in underwater archaeology.

There were five ships in all, and they lay in a shallow part of Roskilde Fjord. They had been scuttled in the middle of the eleventh century at the narrowest part of the main navigation channel to block the fjord and protect the town of Roskilde from attack by Norwegian Viking pirates. The five ships had been filled with stones to make them sink and keep them in position; they were a longship, a light warship, a ferry boat, a small merchantman, and a deep-sea trader, and the weight of the stones over the centuries had gradually flattened out the sodden timbers and made them shapeless.

One of the problems of underwater archaeology is that timber that has been immersed in water for a long time starts warping and crumbling when it is brought to the surface and exposed to the air. This is because the action of the water destroys the cellulose that binds the fabric of the wood. Prompt chemical treatment is essential if the wood is to be preserved, and this treatment is long, laborious and expensive. Each timber has to be immersed for a year or more

in a tank of warm synthetic wax to replace the lost cellulose; and while the water content of the wood is gradually lessened, the wax impregnates the wood instead until it is fully stabilised again.

Once the Danes had decided to try to salvage all the wrecks, they built a coffer dam round the area of the blockage and pumped out the water, leaving the ships deep in a bed of wet sludge; it would have been dangerous to let the timbers be exposed and dry out.

The site had to be kept permanently wet. As the mud was cleared away, the position of the timbers was recorded photogrammetrically before they were prised loose and taken away in hermetically sealed plastic bags.

From a close study of the positions and sizes of the surviving timbers (some seventy per cent of the deep-sea trader had been preserved, for instance), the archaeologists were able to work out what the ships had been like originally. There were literally thousands of fragments—but they were all going to be fitted together again in five huge jigsaw puzzles.

When the timbers had been treated with wax for a year, they had to be re-shaped to their original form. A mould was made for every plank; then each timber was heated in an oven until it was as soft as putty, and pressed into shape on its mould. When it cooled it was ready to be used for building up the ship again.

The five ships are all being treated and restored in a new museum at Roskilde that cost a quarter of a million pounds. The museum workshop is open to the public and is a great attraction; every day, the timbers can be seen being re-shaped and then riveted into place on the hull of one of the ships.

The first ship to be rebuilt was the deep-sea trader, and for a special reason: this was the first example of a deep-sea Viking ship ever found, of the kind that made the long ocean voyages to Iceland and North America five hundred years before Columbus. Seeing the ship in the flesh, as it were, makes a very striking impression—to be able to feel the actual timbers with their original chisel marks and to note the beautiful swan's breast of the prow that the Viking shipwrights had designed by eye alone.

In the case of this particular boat, the archaeologists have managed to piece together, too, an account of her individual history. She was built, not in Denmark, but in Norway, because she was made of pine, not oak; but her keel planking had been severely damaged on one occasion, and she had been repaired with oak—therefore in Denmark. What was she doing in Roskilde? The Danes

Members of Robert Stenuit's diving team with some of the coins they salvaged from the wreck of the *Girona*.

95

had no use for this kind of ocean-going boat, for all their trading was done in the Baltic. Near the prow, however, there are two small arrow-holes, which were made from the outside; and from this one can speculate that the boat had been in a fight some time. Add to this the fact that she was not very old when she was scuttled, and all the clues are gathered for the reconstruction. The archaeologists reasoned that she had been built by the Norwegians for the long North Sea crossing to Iceland and North America, early in the eleventh century. But she seems to have been ambushed by the Danes, in the Skagerrak perhaps, and after a brief battle she was captured and taken home in triumph to Roskilde. She was carelessly beached, and had to be extensively repaired in Roskilde shipyard; but even so she was of little practical use to the Danish merchants of Roskilde; so when danger loomed, and Norwegian pirates prowled the fjord, the sturdy deep-sea trader from the Iceland run, prize of war, was one of the five ships to be sacrificed to make a barrier.

THE PALACE AT FISHBOURNE

There has been a lot of new thinking about the way in which objects, once recovered, should be displayed. The rebuilding of the Viking ships in Roskilde Museum is an impressive example, and it attracted 150,000 visitors to this small town in its first year. Museums are no longer dusty, echoing mausoleums full of ugly glass cases—'ghastly charnel houses of murdered evidence', as Flinders Petrie once called them.

The recent excavation and display in England of the Roman palace at Fishbourne, in Sussex, brilliantly exemplifies the new techniques.

The story began one afternoon in April 1960, when a workman digging a trench for a water-main through a field north of the village of Fishbourne sliced across a mass of Roman tiles. He had the good sense and alertness to examine what he had turned up and report it to his foreman, who in turn reported it to the local archaeological society. Professor Barry Cunliffe of Southampton University was called in, and in seven seasons of concentrated work, from 1961 to 1967, he laid bare the most spectacular Roman palace site in Britain, the largest Roman palace outside Rome—a huge six-acre building that had apparently been presented to a native collaborator, a British king called Tiberius Claudius Cogidubnus, in the first century AD.

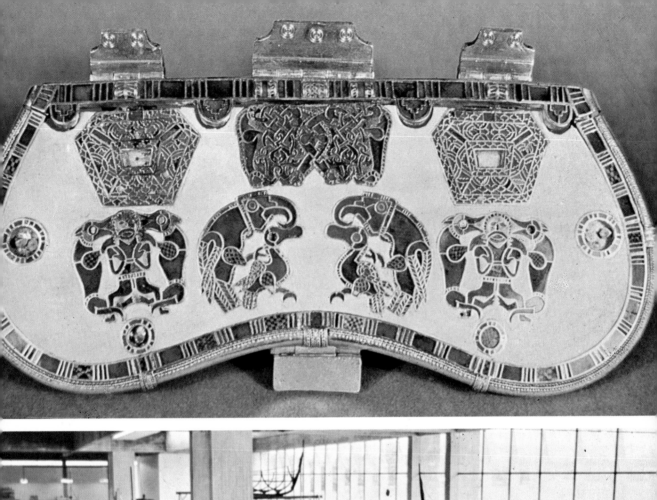

Above Aerial photograph of the hill fort at South Cadbury, the latest claimant to the title of King Arthur's Camelot.
Below The temples at Abu Simbel after their reconstruction.

The palace was built like a vast villa with pillared courts and magnificent mosaic floors. It had underfloor heating that was added later, when the occupants realised that the climate was not as Mediterranean as the architecture. There was a complex of public buildings and a wing of private suites for the king and his guests, and there were splendidly laid-out gardens. This palace lasted for about two hundred years, showing considerable changes and adaptations as the political situation changed, until it was destroyed by fire *c*. 270 AD.

The discovery of a palace on this scale was an event of great importance. But what has immeasurably enhanced it is the way in which it is now displayed to the public. The Chichester Civic Society and the Sussex Archaeological Society raised some £200,000 to build a museum literally on top of the site. The *Sunday Times* newspaper provided design and graphics experts to advise on the layout and display of the objects. And now Fishbourne has a museum that attracts 250,000 members of the public a year.

Information is imparted at two levels—dramatic displays for the uncommitted, and more detailed blocks of information for the committed. The visitor is never left in any doubt as to where to go next; he is metaphorically taken by the hand and led along a narrative history of Roman Britain, all illustrated with visual aids, and from there he goes out onto walkways that give him an aerial view, under cover, of the wonderful mosaic floors.

Instead of massed showcases of finds from the site, selected objects found at Fishbourne are given their proper context in the story of the excavation and the story of Roman Britain. To fill out the story, the designers used copies and casts of material from other museums, such as a copy of the British Museum bust of Vespasian who might once, before he became Emperor, have used Fishbourne as a temporary base, or part of the frieze of Trajan's column (presented by the Italian government), depicting Roman soldiers being transported by water—the way in which the invaders probably attacked Fishbourne in the early stages of the Roman Conquest. There is a replica of a relief of a Roman butcher's shop from the Dresden Museum to illustrate the kind of trading that went on at Fishbourne. Fishbourne Museum has taken the old adage to heart— it instructs by telling a story that can be clearly understood by its visitors.

A new concept of a
museum. Visitors to
Fishbourne can walk
above the mosaic floors
which have been
cleared and then left
in situ.

THE TEMPLES AT ABU SIMBEL

Nowadays archaeology is under severe pressure. Massive modern
developments like motorways and new towns are eating up land at a
frightening rate; and all that land has history beneath it that ought
to be recorded if not preserved. Sometimes it is not possible to
salvage a threatened monument; but there have been some spectacular cases of snatching success from disaster—and none was more
spectacular than the saving of Abu Simbel.

The twin temples at Abu Simbel are the largest rock-cut temples
in the world, gouged out of the sandstone cliffs which dominate the
River Nile near the borders of Egypt and the Sudan. It was built by
the Pharaoh Ramesses II and is decorated with friezes of his
campaign in 1285 BC against the Hittites which culminated in the
Battle of Kadesh, on the northern border of Palestine. In the friezes
on the walls of Abu Simbel, this military debacle was converted into
an impressive victory for the Pharaoh! Four seventy-foot statues of
Ramesses formed the facade of the larger temple, which reached two
hundred feet into the hillside, through courts flanked by pillared
statues of Ramesses, again and again. Abu Simbel was one of the
most remarkable constructions of antiquity.

When the Aswan High Dam was built, 175 miles downstream, the
temples of Abu Simbel were threatened. They would be drowned in

OPPOSITE
Work starting on the
rock temples at Abu
Simbel as the level of
the Nile began to rise.

the artificial reservoir that built up behind the dam. The temples that the Italian giant, Belzoni, had rediscovered under the sand in 1817 would be lost to the world again, this time for ever.

With the help of an international campaign financed by UNESCO, at a cost of 36 million dollars, the temples were saved; they were carved from the living rock into massive blocks and rebuilt piece by piece on the hill-top, two hundred feet above, out of reach of the waters of the Nile.

The sheer engineering problems involved in such an operation are staggering. The whole top of the cliff, some 300,000 tons of rock, had to be sliced off to expose the temple interiors, so that they could be prised out of the mountain in sections. Skilled quarrymen from the great marble quarries of Carrara in Italy were imported for the delicate task of hand-cutting the sandstone statues into manageable blocks. Most of the labourers were Egyptian, but the technicians and civil engineers came from Sweden and fourteen other countries.

Part of a head of Ramesses II has been cut away for transportation to the new site.

When all the 1035 blocks had been taken to the top, they were re-assembled in a vast jigsaw puzzle where every measurement had to be exact to the last millimetre; for the larger temple had been built in such a way that twice a year, and only twice, the first rays of the rising sun would strike full down the length of the temple courts and illuminate four stone gods in the innermost sanctuary. The foundation stone, the first of the blocks, was laid in January 1966; the last of the blocks of the second temple was slotted into place in October. Two years later the last of the rock-scaping was completed, and the temples were open to the public again.

It was a colossal operation, and one that will probably never be matched. But it illustrates the scale of the problems that man's technological progress in the second half of the twentieth century is creating for the world's antiquities—and man's capacity to meet that challenge.

7

Science in Archaeology

The most revolutionary scientific technique to have been developed for archaeological purposes since World War II has been the discovery of the principle of radiocarbon dating. It emerged in the late 1940s as a by-product of atomic research at the Institute of Nuclear Studies in the University of Chicago; the man who discovered it, Professor Willard F. Libby, was awarded the Nobel Prize for its chemical aspects.

Its significance was that it provided archaeologists, for the first time, with a calendar for the remote past, a way of translating time into dates: a means of absolute dating independent of subjective interpretations and relative areas like Stone Age and Bronze Age eras and so on.

Radiocarbon dating, or $C14$ dating as it is often called, works on the basic principle that by measuring the radioactivity of the remains of organic matter, one can estimate the number of years that have elapsed since such organic matter was alive.

The method depends on the fact that there is a certain proportion of radioactive carbon ($C14$) in the carbon dioxide of the atmosphere. It is produced when atoms of nitrogen 14 ($N14$) in the upper atmosphere are bombarded by cosmic rays from outer space. This radioactive 'heavy' carbon of atomic weight 14 mixes with the ordinary carbon ($C12$) in atmospheric carbon dioxide, and thereafter behaves in exactly the same way. Carbon dioxide is one of the great sources of life, an essential element in the process of photosynthesis; it is absorbed by all green plants, and since all animal life is ultimately sustained by plant life, it means that carbon (both $C14$ and $C12$) is incorporated in all living organic matter. During the active life of any living thing, the proportion it contains of radioactive carbon (C14) is minute, but it is maintained at a constant level and it is measurable; it reflects exactly the proportion of C14 to C12 in the atmosphere.

Once organic matter dies, however, it ceases to absorb any further amounts of carbon; the radioactive C14 is no longer replaced as it decays and dwindles. The rate of decay is extremely slow, but it too is known and measurable, so that by measuring how much radio-activity there is left it is possible to tell how long it is since the organism died and stopped absorbing fresh C14.

The way in which this rate of decay is usually expressed is in terms of the so-called 'half-life' of the radioactive element—the time it takes for *half* of the radiocarbon content to decay, which is something like 5,600 or 5,700 years. Thus, every 5,600 or 5,700 years (no one is quite sure about the exact time) the amount of C14 contained in dead organic matter will halve; matter containing *half* the original amount of C14 will thus be 5,600 years old or so, matter containing a *quarter* of the original amount will be 11,200 years old or so, and so on.

The way in which the measurement is made is to compare the proportion of C14 to C12 in the sample being studied with the proportion in a more modern control sample. There are a number of laboratories throughout the world now that can assay the age of samples for archaeological purposes, but it is a highly skilled and specialised operation. First, the sample is thoroughly cleaned with hydrochloric acid to remove inorganic or surface carbonate con-tamination. Thereafter it is sealed in a silica tube and put in a silica furnace, where it is burned in a stream of oxygen which converts all its carbon content back into carbon dioxide. A number of purification processes involving barium hydroxide and barium carbonate follow; when the purification is complete, the carbon dioxide is placed in an anti-radiation chamber to protect it from outside cosmic interference, and the radioactivity of the carbon content is then measured radiometrically inside the lead-brick shield.

The kind of organic matter that can be dated by this method is very varied. Charcoal is perhaps the easiest to deal with, because it is principally composed of carbon. Wood and peat are also relatively simple. Bone and antler, however, contain only a small amount of carbon, principally in the collagen fibres, and the dating process is more complicated—the inorganic matrix has to be removed by acid first, reducing the sample to a sludge, and it is sometimes difficult to get a sample that is sufficiently large. Most plant material is suitable; so too is much of the debris commonly to be found on archaeological sites of various kinds—pieces of rope, seeds, grain, textiles, hair, parchment, paper, even marine shells and freshwater snails, as well as organic soils and mud if the sample is large enough.

Radiocarbon dates are expressed in terms of elapsed years, and are always given a standard deviation to allow for statistical probability: thus, an archaeologist who sends off a sample of wood for dating may get back the answer in this form—4000± (plus or minus) 200. This simply means that there is a 2 to 1 chance (66 per cent probability) that the correct age lies within that bracket of 3,800–4,200 years, and a 93 per cent probability that it lies within twice that range (3,600–4,400 years). Although the layman tends to say simply 'about 4,000 years old' or 'about 2000 BC', the archaeologist will always give the full plus-or-minus figure. So although radiocarbon dating gave archaeologists for the first time the chance to give a precise date to sites outside Egypt as opposed to an estimated position within a framework of eras, it cannot be as precise as historical calendar dating. Even so, it has been a great boon for laymen who are used to a framework of dates in their reading of history, and prefer to think of the Norman Conquest as beginning in 1066 AD rather than in the Early Middle Ages. It is easier to comprehend the date of the Great Pyramid at Giza as being 'about 2270 BC', rather than 'in the Fourth Dynasty of the Old Kingdom'. Radiocarbon dates cannot be as specific as calendar dates; but at least they point to the right century.

It may, however, be necessary now to rethink some of the claims for radiocarbon dating. For the past few years, more and more difficulties have been coming to light. The process is very difficult and delicate, and even the smallest amount of contamination by modern carbon can seriously distort the age-determination. The doubt about the exact length of the 'half-life' of $C14$, on which the rate of decay is based, has created some dubiety about the accuracy of the figures; the original figure of 5,568 years is now thought to be too small, but the amended figure of 5,730 has not been generally agreed yet. Most serious of all, however, it is possible that the fundamental assumption that underlies the whole technique may be suspect—the belief that the rate of production of $C14$ has always been constant. Recently the British Museum carried out a systematic dating programme on a large number of Egyptian tombs whose calendar dates are known. $C14$ tests were carried out on specially

The densely packed rings on this cross-section of a bristlecone pine show an annual record of several thousand years.

collected organic material from these tombs, mostly reeds from the ceilings. These showed that there were serious discrepancies between the known calendar dates and the radiocarbon dates.

These discrepancies could be expressed on a graph as a curve of error, amounting at some periods to several centuries. It also became apparent that there were marked fluctuations at certain times within that curve, caused by variations in the radiocarbon concentration in the organic material. There is still no general agreement about what caused these variations; differing schools of thought suggest solar activity affecting cosmic rays, or the climate, or changing intensities of the earth's geometric field.

Generally speaking, although radiocarbon dates match known calendar dates fairly closely for the past 2,000 years, the discrepancy starts to become serious from then on. This suggests that in the pre-Christian era there was much more carbon 14 being produced naturally than now, and so the radiocarbon dates given are much later than the true calendar-year dates.

One method by which radiocarbon dates can be checked and calibrated against 'true' dates is *dendrochronology*—the technique of dating by tree-rings. It is based on the simple fact that trees grow by adding a growth-ring to their trunks every year. These rings are visible in cross-section, and the age of a tree can be given exactly by counting the number of tree-rings it has grown. Furthermore, if the climate is variable, the growth-rings vary in size; in dry years the rings are thin and meagre, in wet years they are thicker. These growth-rings are also visible on any piece of hewn or dressed wood. In any given area, the tree-rings can be matched into a pattern of alternating dry and wet cycles, if enough samples of timber can be collected; the inside rings of a twentieth-century tree will match the outside rings of a nineteenth-century tree, and so on. Thereafter timber found on archaeological sites can be fitted into this pattern of dates; or else 'floating chronologies' may occur which only need one or two further discoveries to be made in order to be linked into their proper place in the overall pattern.

Everything depends on establishing a master-pattern for each region, and obviously it would be ideal if one could find a very ancient tree in each place to supply that master-pattern. The giant sequoia tree from Sierra Nevada grows to an age of some 3,000 years, which gives a local pattern of tree-rings back to about 1250 BC; and that pattern can be extended by linking up earlier 'floating' chronologies.

Recently, though, a much longer series of tree-ring dates has been prepared from an ugly, warped tree that grows in the White Mountains of east-central California called the bristlecone pine (*pinus longaeva*). Its great value to archaeology is that it grows to an immense age owing to the peculiar climatic conditions of the area; trees as old as 5,000 years have been found. Beyond this age limit, dead parts of bristlecone pine have been found that have allowed scientists to trace a continuous record of tree-rings back to 6300 BC, and some other pieces of wood seem to be another 2,000 years older than that.

At the Tree Ring Research Laboratory at Tucson, Arizona, scientists have been making radiocarbon determinations on the wood from this tree and comparing them with the known date derived from counting the growth-rings. From this it has been possible to compile a chart showing how the radiocarbon dates differed from the true dates, and it became clear that the discrepancy grew from about 200 years at 1500 BC to 700 years at 3500 BC. The size of the discrepancy roughly matched the experience gained from the radiocarbon analysis of Egyptian tomb material.

The effect of this on conventional archaeological thinking is profound. It means that all dates for the Stone Age have to be set earlier than was supposed, by several centuries; and this can gravely disturb accepted theories. For instance: in the past it has been assumed, on the basis of radiocarbon dating and cross-dating, that the period of the latest work on Stonehenge, the so-called Wessex Culture of the British Bronze Age, had had some sort of cultural or inspirational links with the Golden Age of Mycenae, around 1500 BC. But the new corrected dates for this Stonehenge period may now be 2000 BC or even earlier, so the Wessex-Mycenae link will have to be re-assessed. Indeed, our whole thinking about cultural influences will have to be re-assessed; it is now clear, for instance, that the prehistoric giant temples of Malta are older than the pyramids, and therefore could not have been influenced by them. Similarly, the 700-year shift means that some things like metallurgy which were thought to have originated in the east and been brought to Europe by a process known as cultural diffusion may indeed have originated in Europe quite independently.

There are various other scientific techniques for computing age. In Scandinavia, scientists have developed a system known as *varve-dating*, which works on roughly the same principle as dendro-chronology but is applied to the annual melting of ice. The method is basically geological. Each spring, when it thaws, the rivers bring down from the glacial regions huge quantities of debris that are deposited in lakes or estuaries; and later each summer, when the force of the current is lessened, smaller, finer soils and gravels are carried down and deposited. Each year's layer of sediment is called a varve and can be read in profile, just like a tree ring pattern of wet and dry years. This *geochronology*, as it is called, is based on finding overlapping patterns to build up a coherent picture stretching back to the end of the last Ice Age—about 12,000 years; and although it is not nearly so accurate as tree-ring dating, archaeological sites can sometimes be plotted into the pattern.

Another specialised technique borrowed from geology is that of *tephrachronology*, which is the dating of ash-layers, or layers of tephra, from volcanic eruptions. Where historical records of destructive eruptions exist, this technique can be used to give a very precise date to sites that were destroyed by volcanic activity. In Iceland, for instance, it was used to give an exact date (1104 AD) to a well preserved Viking Age manor at Stöng in Thjórsárdale that had been smothered by volcanic fall-out from Mount Hekla.

Two double-headed vessels of the Hacilar style from Anatolia in Turkey. The one on the left has been proved to be genuine, having thermoluminescence consistent with its presumed origin in the 6th millenium BC. The one on the right has been proved to have been made recently, having negligible thermoluminescence.

The most recent innovation in dating techniques is known as *thermoluminescence*. This is a means of dating artifacts, particularly pottery, by measuring the amount of radioactive decay that has taken place since the artifact was fired. The firing of pottery wipes the slate clean, as it were, and creates a completely new structure which starts to age from that moment onwards. After firing, flaws in the lattice of the mineral crystals of the pottery trap alpha-particles through radioactivity, and if the pottery is re-heated these alpha-particles will be released in the form of light-energy which can be measured. This allows the time since the pottery was last heated to be calculated. It is still a rather imprecise technique; but since it can be used on the commonest artifact in archaeology, it gives great promise for the future as an eventual check on radiocarbon dating of organic materials.

Fluorine testing is a method which can be applied to bone that has been buried for a long time. It depends on the fact that when bones lie in the ground, the phosphoric calcium is very slowly replaced by the fluorine element in the moisture that percolates the sand or gravel in which they lie. The rate at which this happens varies according to the dampness of the site; but broadly speaking the greater the fluorine content the older the bone. Fluorine testing has proved useful in assessing whether bones found scattered in gravel deposits are associated with one another.

Before deciding where to start excavating, an archaeologist can gain much useful information by using an appliance such as the *proton magnetometer* to detect soil anomalies beneath the surface. It is only one of many such instruments—the gradiometer, for instance, or the bleeper which was developed from it, or the telohm, or the megger earth tester. The magnetometer measures the intensity of the earth's magnetic field; since topsoil is more magnetic than subsoil, then pits and ditches will show up as anomalies in the general pattern. So, obviously, will buried metal. Other instruments measure differences in the resistance to the passage of an electric current. These differences usually depend on the amount of water present under the surface; an area which was once disturbed to make a pit will tend to be more waterlogged than its undisturbed surroundings, and therefore offer less resistance than, say, a large stone wall. Some remarkably precise configurations can be plotted with the help of instruments of this nature; during the 1960's, the location and even street-plan of the long-sunken city of Sybaris in southern Italy was revealed by extensive surveys by a proton magnetometer.

Aerial photography can be another invaluable aid, pioneered by the eminent British archaeologist O. G. S. Crawford (d. 1958). In post-war years it has been greatly developed by Dr J. K. St Joseph of Cambridge. Photographs taken from the air can often reveal the most astonishing and unexpected features in the ground. In low sunlight, exaggerated shadow marks can point up the presence of imperceptible relief patterns. Ancient features can also be seen as crop marks: a field of ripening corn will show a 'shadow' of where ancient ditches were dug or old buildings once stood because of the different soils that have accumulated over them. Corn, for instance, grows shorter over buried road surfaces or wall foundations, and longer over once-dug ditches. In the same way, echoes of ancient paths and walls will be apparent on a field covered with snow, and vanished villages will show through a cover of vegetation as if behind a veil.

One further scientific development requires mention, as showing how archaeology has broadened from the narrow business of finding and studying the relics of man. *Palaeobotany*—the study of ancient plant remains—seeks to build up a picture of early man's environment and his effect on it. Charcoal can be studied and identified, for each wood has a different structure, to show what kind of trees grew near human settlements and what use man made of this important resource. But the most important element of palaeobotany is *pollen analysis* (palynology). The millions of tiny grains of pollen shed by trees and plants are remarkably resistant to decay, and can survive for thousands of years. Under a microscope, they can be identified by pollen analysts; sometimes even the individual species can be recognised. From this, a picture of the vegetation of an area during specific prehistoric periods can be built up. By taking samples from different levels of an excavation, the botanist can produce a profile of the changing character of the land, showing how woodlands slowly developed after the end of the Ice Age and how pasture and arable land came into use at particular periods.

The botanical profile sometimes enables the archaeologist to date a site, by fitting it into the known pattern of vegetational change. It can also tell us a great deal about the culture of the human beings involved. A sharp decline in the proportion of tree pollen, with a corresponding rise in the proportion of grasses and crops, indicates when early man started clearing forests and grazing animals or planting cereals. Thus the botanist joins the ranks of scientists who are helping the archaeologist to fill in as large a picture as possible of Man's past in the broadest sense.

8

Illicit Archaeology

One field in particular in which science has come to the aid of
archaeology is in detecting forgeries. Anti-forgery weapons are now
extremely sophisticated. One of them is an instrument called the
microprobe, which is based on that dramatic scientific invention of
the 1960's, the *laser*. The laser (short for Light Amplification by
Stimulated Emission of Radiation) is a device straight out of the
pages of science fiction; it was H. G. Wells in *The War of the Worlds*
in 1898 who first armed the invading Martians with a mysterious
'sword of heat' from which flickered 'a ghost of a beam of light'
which could melt lead and slice through anything. Now the laser,
invented less than a decade ago, can do that and more.

The basic principle of the laser is that it shoots out a narrow,
highly concentrated beam of sharp, intense light; and the value of
the microprobe to archaeology is that it permits quick and easy
analysis of an object without doing it serious damage. One burst of a
laser beam vaporises an infinitesimal amount of material (as little as
a millionth of an ounce), leaving only a tiny crater. This vaporised
material, further heated by an electric spark, rises in a plume whose
light is read by a spectrograph which breaks down the light into a
spectrum of its component colours and photographs it. Lines on this
spectrum identify the chemical elements involved.

The first object to be tested by the microprobe was an alleged
sixteenth-century Flemish painting at the Museum of Fine Arts in
Boston. When it was X-rayed the scientific curator became suspic-
ious because the X-rays passed through too easily—they should have
been blocked by the lead carbonate that was used in sixteenth-
century pigments. A laser-spectrogram showed a series of dark lines

that indicated the presence of zinc, and with that the picture was conclusively proved to be a forgery, because zinc was never used in painters' pigments until 1820.

With such potent scientific aids available, it is hard to see how a forgery can ever be accepted or remain undetected for very long. And yet forgeries still occur with remarkable regularity, and they still succeed for a time—perhaps because people at heart want to be deceived if the deception happens to suit their own hopes or ideas.

In the year 1908, a respectable English solicitor called Charles Dawson found a fragment of what appeared to be a fossilised human skull in a gravel pit at Piltdown, near Brighton in Sussex. This find, and other pieces of bone that were found nearby over the next few years, aroused enormous interest, because it came at a time when the whole scientific world was afire with theories about Early Man. Darwin's theory of evolution and the discovery in 1856 of primitive man-remains at Neanderthal in Germany had started the hunt for the Missing Link between ape and humans that Darwin had postulated. It was in this somewhat fevered atmosphere of scientific speculation that Piltdown Man made his debut.

The Piltdown site. From right to left Dawson, Smith Woodward and Veness Hargreaves their chief helper. Chipper, the goose, usually came to the site when Dawson was at work.

The first find, the left cranial bone of a fossilised human skull, was made by Dawson, who was an enthusiastic amateur geologist. Three years later, in the same place, he found part of the forehead and back skull. Later, various distinguished visitors came across further fragments, in particular part of a lower jaw with teeth in it—this find was made by the distinguished English anthropologist Smith Woodward. What was so startling about the finds was that the skull was recognisably human, without even the heavy brow-bones of Neanderthal Man—but the jaw was distinctly ape-like. Dawson and Smith Woodward, and soon the whole world of science, acclaimed the skull as being that of Piltdown Man—half man, half ape, the long-lost Missing Link, some 500,000 years old; and a grateful public named him *Eoanthropus Dawsoni*—'Dawson's Dawn Man'.

But were the fragments genuine? Argument was to rage for nearly fifty years: that jaw, it was claimed, could not possibly belong to that cranium. But Smith Woodward remained convinced. The specimens were kept under close guard in the Museum of Natural History in London, and no specialists were allowed to touch them. After the Second World War, however, two British anthropologists were allowed to make some proper scientific tests—in particular, the Fluorine Test. And in 1953 the 'Oldest Englishman', as he had been proudly called, was revealed as a fraud. The skull fragments had a high fluorine content of 0·1 per cent, which indicated an age of several thousand years, and were proved to be from the cranium of *homo sapiens*. But the fluorine content of that controversial lower jaw turned out to be a mere 0·03 per cent. It was the jaw-bone of an extremely modern orang-utan.

Once the fraud had been revealed, a lot of things were revealed that should have come to light earlier. The jawbone had been deliberately broken and stained brown with potassium bichromate to make it look old; but the colour was only on the surface. The teeth embedded in the jaw were now seen to have been filed down with an iron file, to make it look more human. The animal remains that had been found in association with the alleged human remains were of widely scattered origins; and various flint tools that had been found nearby were now seen to have been shaped with an iron knife.

And so the theory of Piltdown Man was discredited. Suspicion fell on Charles Dawson; but he may have been as much of a victim as everybody else. It should not be forgotten that all this happened at a time when Cambridge University was celebrated for its practical jokes, and that a museum there unaccountably lost a fossilised human skull that year. But whoever was responsible, it was certainly one of the most celebrated and successful hoaxes in the history of archaeology.

Why did it succeed for so long? How did it manage to convince and deceive so many of the world's most eminent scientists for forty years? The answer probably is that people, no matter how intelligent and educated, tend to believe what they want to believe, for personal, professional, or even patriotic reasons. In that frame of mind they are ready victims for the forger. Also, collectors with a greed for owning 'discoveries' provide a market for the forgers when the demand outstrips the supply of genuine finds. One thing is common to all successful forgeries: they only happen when there is a ready-made market, a public appetite for new discovery.

One of the most exciting stories in the history of exploration is the account given in the Icelandic Sagas of the discovery and attempted settlement of North America (Vínland) by the Vikings around the year 1000 AD, 500 years before Christopher Columbus. Many people have considered it a fable, but this was mainly due to a misunderstanding of the nature of the Sagas; modern scholars now recognise that the Sagas also have historical validity to a greater or lesser degree, and see no reason to doubt the authenticity of the tradition of Viking discoveries in the west. In the past, however, there has never been any concrete archaeological evidence for the presence of the Vikings on North American soil; so the evidence was faked instead.

In 1898, a farmer called Olof Ohman was felling a tree at his home near Kensington in the state of Minnesota when, he claimed, he found a huge stone slab enmeshed in its roots. The stone was 82 centimetres high, 40 centimetres broad; and it was inscribed with what purported to be runic letters. The inscription read:

'. . . 8 Goths and 22 Norwegians on an expedition from Vinland to the west. Our camp was by 2 skerries a day's journey north from this stone. We went fishing one day. When we came home found 10 men red with blood and dead. AVM (Ave Maria) deliver us from evil. Have 10 men by the sea to look after our ships 14 days' journey from this island. 1362.'

Runes were the ancient Germanic alphabet that was used for inscriptions and magic incantations before the introduction of the Roman alphabet and writing on paper; and this inscription clearly suggested that Scandinavian adventurers were still busy exploring

North America 350 years after the first Vikings had gone there, and that they had penetrated deep into the heart of the continent.

The foremost Scandinavian scholars of the day refused to accept the stone as being genuine, saying that the language was much too modern and the rune-writing faulty. But one scholar, Hjalmar R. Holand, bought it for 25 dollars and spent the rest of his life trying to prove its authenticity. Eventually, after a stream of articles and essays by him, the Smithsonian Institute of the National Museum in Washington accepted it and put it on display, and the State of Minnesota set up a Rune Stone Memorial Park with a three-ton granite replica of the Stone as its centrepiece.

The Kensington Stone has now been proved conclusively to be not just a forgery but a ludicrously bad forgery. The runic language used in it is nonsensical, imitated from a Swedish runic calendar of the eighteenth century, one of the letters was a pure invention, and the grammatical forms were incorrect. The man who claimed to have found the stone was an immigrant from Sweden who lived in the most Swedish state in the USA. He swore that he knew nothing about runes, but after his death a teach-yourself book was found amongst his belongings with a well-thumbed chapter on the development of Swedish from the runic to the modern language.

Oddly enough there are still people who believe the Kensington Stone to be genuine—or rather, who want to believe it. The Americans have always wanted to find out about their own pre-history, and Scandinavian immigrants have always been anxious to prove their own notable part in that prehistory. In the eighteen-nineties there was particular interest in both Scandinavia and America about the Viking discovery of Vínland; only five years before the Stone was found, the newspapers were full of stories about the sea-crossing from Bergen to Newfoundland that was made in 1893 by a replica of the handsome Viking boat found at Gokstad, in Norway. So the stage was set for forgery, and a forgery duly appeared.

In recent years, two further claims have been made concerning authentic evidence of the Viking presence in North America. In 1965, a previously unknown medieval map purporting to show 'Vínland' came to light in mysterious circumstances; it was bought by Yale University from a dealer who could not, or would not, reveal details of where it had come from. It was claimed to be a map of the world, made in Basle, Switzerland, around 1440, some fifty years before Columbus set sail for the west.

The Kensington Stone.

The other claim concerns an archaeological site at a place called L'Anse au Meadows, in the north of Newfoundland. Although the excavation has not yet been published in full, the ruins appear to be of Norse origin, and radiocarbon dates ranging from 700–1080 AD seem to confirm this conclusion.

It is too early to say yet whether these claims can be proved. But caution requires us to remember that early in the 1960s there was an upsurge of scholarly interest in the whole subject of Vínland following some important textual studies on the relationship between the Sagas concerned.

Some frauds, when they are discovered, prove to be so blatant and so reckless that it is hard to believe that they could ever have deceived anyone. Yet for three years, a young ploughman in France kept up an astonishing output of forged antiquities from an excavation site that was under constant attention from scientists and newspapers.

On March 1st 1924, a fifteen-year-old farmboy called Emile Fradin, from the village of Glozel near Vichy in France, was ploughing a field with his oxen when the animals stumbled into a depression in the ground. Fradin found two bricks with twisted designs incised on them, and later that evening he uncovered at a depth of 80 centimetres a paved floor, some fragments of glass, and a genuine Neolithic polished stone axe-head. The presence of the axe-head was coincidence; for what Fradin had stumbled on were the remains of a medieval glassmaker's brick furnace. The local school-mistress, however, mistakenly identified it as an incineration grave; and this was the start of a fraud that was to set the whole of France by the ears.

The local schoolmaster was detailed by the learned society of the region to study the find, and he enthusiastically supported the incineration grave theory; he also lent the boy Emile various books on prehistory and archaeology. One or two inscribed pebbles and tiles now made their appearance on the site, but they were tactfully ignored as hoaxes. But then, a year later, an amateur Vichy archaeologist signed a contract for the exclusive excavation rights, and arranged to pay Emile Fradin for any finds that might turn up. Fradin needed no further encouragement; for the next two years, he ensured a constant supply of 'finds'—over 2,000 assorted fragments of unfired clay vessels, pebbles incised with reindeer pictures, urns with faces, clay tablets inscribed with Phoenician characters, bone artifacts—even two 'graves' filled with badly made pots and pieces of human bone from a nearby cemetery.

Today the forgeries are ludicrously obvious. But one scholar had staked his reputation on their authenticity, and on the evidence they provided he had built up a theory that it was Glozel and not the Orient that was the true birthplace of civilisation in Neolithic times. France's honour was at stake, and so was his professional reputation, and he was unlikely to accept the finds as anything but genuine from then on.

Finally the forgeries became so blatant that in 1927 an international commission of archaeologists was appointed to visit the site, make some test digs, and report. On the first day of the dig they found nothing; but overnight some pieces of bone with scratched incisions made their appearance, along with a soft clay tablet covered with Phoenician symbols. The commission reported that they could find nothing of any antiquity at Glozel at all, and now the authorities moved in. A police raid on Fradin's farm disclosed a hoard of half-finished objects, and tablets of clay drying in the rafters of the barn.

The Prehistoric Society thereupon instituted proceedings against an Unknown Person for fraud. Emile Fradin and his neighbour (who had by now also started finding Glozel material on his farm) were prosecuted—for charging entry money without having an entertainments licence. No conviction followed, however; the court ruled that there had certainly been fraud by Person or Persons Unknown, but that Fradin had been perfectly entitled to claim compensation in the shape of entry fees for the loss of time he suffered at the hands of all the thousands of visitors who poured in to see the finds!

At least the locality did well out of it, even if some of the foremost scholars in France had made themselves look ridiculous. Fradin opened a cafe, and the tourist trade boomed as never before; a local baker made a small fortune making *briques néolithiques*—in marzipan!

Forging can be good business. So can the smuggling of stolen antiquities, or antiquities illegally looted from archaeological sites. The problem today is particularly acute in Turkey, where there is a tremendous wealth of material waiting to be excavated, and a hungry market in Europe and the USA ready to buy up anything that comes up for sale. It is well known that there is a thriving black market organised by dealers who are smuggling hundreds of thousands of pounds worth of antiques out of Turkey in direct defiance of the laws of the country regarding archaeological antiquities. It is also well known that all too many western museums who sometimes buy these antiquities will blandly accept the thinnest stories about how they got out of Turkey in the first place.

But the most notorious area for the looting and counterfeiting and smuggling of antiquities in the world of archaeology is probably the field of Etruscan archaeology. Antiquarian interest in the handsome antiquities of Etruscan art started in the sixteenth century and has never diminished. Illicit excavation of Etruscan tombs is a flourishing profession in Italy—and a very professional business too. Greek and Etruscan works fetch high prices on the international market at present.

In Rome there is a thriving market for the work of small-time counterfeiters, who turn out very passable imitations of Etruscan terracotta vases or jewellery to profit from the current vogue for Etruscan art. But there are professional operators of considerable standing as well. In the year 1930, the British Museum was reluct-

One of the terracotta
Etruscan warrior
figures bought by the
Metropolitan Museum
of Art, New York, and
later discovered to be
a forgery.

antly compelled to admit that a handsome Etruscan sarcophagus in terracotta representing the reclining figures of a man and a woman was a clever forgery, copied from the Cerveteri sarcophagus in the Louvre. For nearly fifty years the Metropolitan Museum of Art in New York was deceived over some huge terracotta figures of warriors which had in fact been manufactured in 1914 in Orvieto by a distinguished family of counterfeiters, the Riccardis. Having made the figures, the Riccardis broke them into fragments to make them more convincing, and sold them to the Museum. After the Second World War, scientific examination by spectrograph and other means suggested strongly that the pieces were forgeries; but the argument was not finally settled until one of the accomplices of the Riccardis revealed the whole story of how the forgery had been made.

Ultimately, it is the public who are to blame for the forgeries and the smuggling. If there were not sufficient museums and private collectors prepared to pay high prices for forbidden objects, and if there were not sufficient tourists who wanted to take home a bargain-price trophy, the counterfeiter and the smuggler would cease to exist.

9

Amateur Archaeology

Archaeology today is facing a great challenge. Modern redevelopment is going on at such a pace that archaeologists cannot hope to excavate all the sites that are accidentally revealed by the bulldozer. In every country in the world there is a shortage of trained archaeologists, or rather a shortage of archaeological posts. Too many countries see archaeology as a non-productive activity, and feel they have better things to spend their money on.

In spite of this, archaeology today offers more than ever before as a career, with an exciting range of possible activities. Professional archaeologists insist that it is not nearly such a glamorous job as it is made to sound. Excavation and discovery are only a small part of it, sometimes a very minor part. Most of the work is wearisome and exacting, a matter of meticulous recording and analysing, and many hours in the library. Every season has to be laboriously written up afterwards so that a full account of what was done and noted can be published as soon as possible, for the benefit of other archaeologists.

Nor is it an easy profession to get into. There are very few full-time posts available at present. But students can take archaeology as part of another degree course as well as a principal subject, and the museum service also offers career opportunities without the necessity of a university degree in the lower grades.

But most people will mainly be interested in archaeology as a strictly amateur hobby. In the past, amateurs have contributed in no small way to important finds. Nor is age a barrier. In 1958, for instance, a twelve-year-old Shetland boy called Douglas Coutts who was spending his holidays helping at an excavation on St Ninian's Isle was lucky enough to discover the beautiful hoard of Celtic

Amateur archaeologists at Vindolanda, the Roman fort and settlement in Northumberland, near Hadrian's Wall.

silverware which is now in the National Museum of Antiquities of Scotland in Edinburgh—the greatest single find of Celtic silverware ever made in Scotland. The celebrated cave-paintings of Lascaux in south-western France were discovered in 1940 when five children out rabbiting followed their dog down a hole that had opened up when a winter storm uprooted a tree.

These were fortuitous discoveries, of course. The best way to enjoy archaeology to the full is to try to take part in an excavation. Throughout the country there are local archaeological societies which provide a programme of evening lectures throughout the winter and perhaps organise a properly supervised excavation in the summer. Archaeologists are always happy to accept help from volunteers who are prepared to work hard for no money and take a responsible interest in the dig.

Those who have never been on a dig before may be surprised by all the careful preparatory work that has to be done. The whole site has to be carefully recorded first—photographed, measured, and surveyed. Perhaps there will be an aerial survey made to point up features not immediately apparent at ground level, or a soil survey to try to detect subterranean disturbance.

When the digging starts, there will be no attempt to go straight to where the best prospect of a 'find' might be. The archaeologist is concerned to discover the whole story of an area. If it is a burial mound, he will want to know how the mound was built up, just as much as what is in it, if anything. He will be looking for discarded objects, the unintentional clues left by careless workmen.

The novice will be expected to do a lot of rather tedious work at first. He or she may have to do some heavy spadework, clearing a site of top-soil that will not yield any useful information, sitting washing pieces of broken pottery and making sure they go into the right plastic bag, so that there will be no doubt about where they were found. It may turn out that he or she has a particularly sensitive touch, so the work allocated may be trowelling through the earth, scraping it gently a centimetre at a time to ensure that nothing, however tiny, is lost. And at every stage, the trainee will be taught the paramount importance of patient and accurate observation; he must look for almost imperceptible changes in the colour and texture of the soil, he must be on the alert to stop work at once if something catches his attention. Above all, he must learn to resist the temptation to dig something out by himself in order to be able to brandish it in triumph to his envious colleagues! Careless handling could ruin a fragile object for ever.

Digging can be very hard work indeed, and if it is wet, or even worse, extremely hot, the conditions can become very uncomfortable. But there is the cameraderie of the evenings, after a day's shared hard work. There is the pleasure of feeling one's own skill grow, one's own knowledge and capacity to recognise evidence from the buried past. And sometimes there is the satisfaction of a discovery that will add significantly to the sum of human knowledge— and that makes up for all discomforts.

The one thing the amateur should never try to do is to dig on his own for it is not the find alone that is important—it is the context in which it was found. An object of value gains immeasurably if it is found by a trained archaeologist in the course of a properly and scientifically run excavation.

Those who want to take part in an excavation can find out from their local library how to set about it. In Britain, there is a monthly *Calendar of Excavations*, for instance, which lists all the digs at which volunteers would be welcomed. For those still at school, some local education authorities encourage active participation in digs as a creative form of learning history.

Above all, archaeology is there to be enjoyed; either in books, or in museums, or with spade in hand, one of the most illuminating and enthralling leisure pursuits there is.

123

BOOKS FOR FURTHER READING

There is a large number of books available on every aspect of archaeology. For particular civilisations, the 'Ancient Peoples and Places' series published by Thames and Hudson and edited by Dr Glyn Daniel is invaluable.

This brief list is no more than a handful of suggestions chosen for their availability and general value.

ALBRIGHT, W. F., Archaeology and the Religion of Israel (The John Hopkins Press, Toronto, 1935)

BASS, GEORGE F., Archaeology Under Water (Penguin Books, Harmondsworth 1970)

BIBBY, GEOFFREY, The Testimony of the Spade (Fontana, London 1956)

BRONDSTED, JOHANNES, The Vikings (Pelican Books, Harmondsworth 1965)

BRUCE-MITFORD, R. L. S., The Sutton Hoo Burial Ship (British Museum, London 1968)

CHADWICK, NORA, The Celts (Penguin Books, Harmondsworth 1970)

CORCORAN, J. X. W. P., The Young Field Archaeologist's Guide (G. Bell & Sons, London 1966)

COTTRELL, LEONARD, Lost Cities (Pan Books, London 1957)

CRAWFORD, O. G. S., Archaeology in the Field (J. M. Dent & Sons, London 1953)

DANIEL, GLYN, The Origins and Growth of Archaeology (Penguin Books, Harmondsworth 1967)

Dictionary of Archaeology (Allen Lane, The Penguin Press, London 1970)

HAWKES, J. C., Prehistoric Britain (Penguin Books, Harmondsworth 1958)

MURRAY, M. A., The Splendour that was Egypt (Four Square Books, London 1962)

PAOR, LIAM DE, Archaeology, an Illustrated Introduction (Penguin Books, Harmondsworth 1969)

PIGGOT, STUART, Approach to Archaeology (A. & C. Black, London 1959)

RICHMOND, I. A., Roman Britain (Penguin Books, Harmondsworth 1955)

ROE, DEREK, Prehistory (Paladin, London 1970)

THOMPSON, ERIC S., The Rise and Fall of Maya Civilisation (University of Oklahoma, 1966)

WHEELER, SIR MORTIMER, Archaeology from the Earth (Penguin Books, Harmondsworth 1956)

INDEX